D1396923

Forget Selling

12 Principles of Influence and Persuasion in Sales, Leadership, and Life

Edie Raether

Performance Plus Publishing

Published by:
Performance Plus Publishing
4717 Ridge Water Court
Holly Springs, NC 27540

Additional copies of *Forget Selling*
and other books by the author may be requested by visiting our website at
www.raether.com

Cover design by Michelle Glenn

Library of Congress Cataloging-in-Publication Data
Raether, Edie
      Forget Selling: 12 Principles of Influence and Persuasion in Sales,
           Leadership, and Life — 1st edition
      Includes index.
      ISBN 1-931219-03-6

Dedication

To my beloved mentors and masters of persuasion, my grandchildren:

Zhenya Zhurilo

Seth, Amanda, Grace, Alexander, and Melanie Raether

Contents

Introduction

The power of influence and persuasion has always existed and is certainly not a trendy term. The persuasion skills exhibited by people such as Jesus, Moses, Buddha, Mother Teresa, Martin Luther, President Lincoln, Gandhi, and Martin Luther King offer lessons for all of us. Unfortunately, Osama Bin Laden, Adolf Hitler, Jim Jones, and Saddam Hussein are also master persuaders, not by the use of skilled techniques but by the use of fear and force. The twelve principles contained in this book must never be practiced against another's will, but only for their benefit and self interest as they would define it.

Power is defined as the potential to allocate resources and to make and enforce decisions. It is what you have. Influence is an extension of power in that it is a mechanism through which people use power to change behavior or attitudes and thus it can be described as what you do. Unlike power, influence can produce an effect without the apparent exertion of force, compulsion, or direct command, and is often a two-way street. However, influence can be exerted through manipulation.

Energy is the primary source of influence and power as confirmed in the following by Dr. Robert Cooper, author of *Executive EQ* and a pioneer of emotional intelligence:

> *At its best, emotional intelligence is about influence without manipulation or authority. It's about perceiving, learning, relating, innovating, prioritizing, and acting in ways that take into account emotional valence, rather than relying on logic or intellect or technical analysis alone. Our emotions, as much as or more than our bodies and minds, contain our histories, every line and verse of every experience, deep understanding, and relationship in our lives. They compromise the feeling of who we are and enter our systems as an energy that radiates, that resonates. This energy is the transmitter*

and recorder of all feelings, thoughts, and interactions. In some respects, our biography becomes not only our biology but also our presence in the world.

Few managers would deny that competition is intensifying everywhere in the world. Yet, in more and more cases, the traditional ways to compete—in offers and markets, in customer-centered focus—are getting subsumed by competition through influence...People who are attuned to intuitive information and the uses of emotional intelligence will find that they have more influence than others under the time pressures of today's workplace. Why? In part, because the more analytical five-sensory human focuses principally on exerting influence through the external pursuit of power and control, maneuvering and manipulation. In contrast, with high emotional intelligence, we tend to be more inner directed and can access a wider range of competencies than with cognitive power alone, and this is expressed as a form of influence that might best be called resonance rather than authority...Each attitude, emotion, and action you have—and that others have—creates an influence, a radiance. 'Give the world the best you have and the best will come back to you.'

When you communicate with others, you are continually influencing or being influenced. We are all constantly selling or being sold something, whether it is a product, service, value system, or way of thinking. Although most of the discussion and examples contained in this book are related to business, leadership, and sales, these powerful principles can be applied equally to personal and family relationships.

In America it is believed that some 2.3 trillion dollars of our gross domestic product comes from our ability to influence and persuade others. Indeed, the power of persuasion makes the economic, political, and romantic worlds go around. These essential strategies for producing "yes" each has its own "sway-ability," but when combined with two or more of its sister principles, the grouping creates an irresistible, highly predictable, yet totally voluntary compliance. Thus, these principles must be applied with integrity and in the spirit of serving others. They also require a MindShift™ from traditional, logical/analytical thinking to an intuitive sense of knowing for instant influence. Since the world moves at a faster pace on so many levels, a lot of decision-making is now based on gut feelings. Intuitive intelligence has now become a reliable, more acceptable complement to decision-making and problem solving

Like public speaking, the ability to persuade is a learned skill. While some people seem to be born persuaders, the little known fact is that the majority of those who become experts at influence develop their ability through sweat equity—practice, patience, and persistence. Do not undermine your potential to influence by thinking you are not naturally gifted with persuasive powers.

Although it is often assumed that extroverts are the best persuaders, research reveals that many of the very best change masters are introverts, implying that their gift is rooted in something other than the ability to fast-talk, coerce, and bend the will of others. Their gift is in being genuine, authentic, and caring. President Lincoln, in spite of his depression and lack of confidence, rose to the level of his position and became one of the greatest persuaders of all time as he changed the definition and DNA of freedom. It was his passion in what he believed was best for the Union that motivated him to bring together a divided nation. Desire is everything as illustrated in the following story.

> A Zen Master is out in the woods with his student. Out of nowhere jumps a rabbit scurrying furiously, with a fox chasing him in pursuit of his next meal. Watching the chase, the Zen Master asks the student, "Who will win?" The student quickly replies, "Well, of course, the fox. He is stronger and faster." The Zen Master remains silent for a few moments and then replies, "No, the rabbit will get away." The student is puzzled and admits he does not understand. The Zen Master continues, "The fox is chasing the rabbit for a meal. The rabbit is running for his life." Influence and persuasion is most successful when fueled by desire.

Before you can effectively influence others as a parent, leader, or salesperson, you must first understand what influences you—your purpose, your passion, and your desires. More than any other factor, your personal values influence how you think, feel, and perform. The late Robert S. Hartman, Ph.D., a Nobel Prize nominee, created the science of Axiology which is a mathematical model of a scientific system and objective assessment to measure personal values. If you seem to be recycling your goals, the goal is not the problem—your thinking is. Think before you think! Reflect on how your values have influenced the results you've been getting and what you might do differently to get different results.

There are three levels of value. Intrinsic, the highest order of value, refers to relationships, intuition, and self-esteem. Extrinsic value relates to the tangible, functional, and concrete. Systemic is the lowest order of value and deals with rules, policies, and "shoulds and oughts."

What you want is always influenced by the relative value you place on these three levels of value. By developing balance within these value systems, your thoughts support rather than sabotage your success. To follow are the three essential factors for mastering change:

The Internal System of Influence for Mastering Change

1. Know what you want. Expect it and know that you deserve it.
2. Get out of your own way. Honestly assess where you are going and move forward.
3. Take action now. Start doing what it takes to start getting what you want.

Influence and persuasion begin with making decisions that reflect our internal programming and how we are "hardwired." To effectively persuade others you must understand both how you and those you influence organize their thinking and emotions to make value judgments. Your tendencies become talents when nurtured by a supportive environment. Often times outside influences cause confusion and internal conflict which is why personal alignment is crucial to your personal and professional success. You will become a master of persuasion only when you have liberated yourself from your own outside influences and internal distractions. To unleash your PowerZone™ go to www.raether.com.

Forget Selling reflects win-win interactions requiring influence with integrity, passion, and compassion. These twelve principles explain that making a sale is not just about what or how well you sell, but how others buy. Selling is not selling, but buying a piece of another's mind. Skillfully applying these principles will make the difference between hoping for success and having success.

Overview
The DNA of Influence and Persuasion

*The only way on earth to influence the other fellow is to talk about
what he wants and show him how to get it.*
Dale Carnegie

As you read this book, reflect on how you might apply each nugget
of knowledge to your role as parent, partner, leader, manager, or sales
person. Think BIG, for the size of your thinking will determine the level
of your success. Influence and persuasion are all about getting results
and persuading others to act in their own best interest.

As Dave Yoho, author of *Managing Yourself and Others,* explained,
"A true test of strong management is how well you convince others to do
that which is in their own best interest...The measure of all communication
is the outcome. If you are not getting the outcomes you want, change
your pattern of communication... We meet seemingly charismatic
personalities whose major skill in outperforming their contemporaries
was directly related to their ability to influence and persuade those whom
they managed in such a manner as to exceed goals and outperform other
similar groups. We discovered that they appealed to very basic human
drives and needs found in those people and applied their persuasive skills
in such an easily understood manner as to get immediate results."

Persuasion Changes Behaviors with Voluntary Compliance

Persuasion is a process through which one aims to change or reinforce
the attitudes, opinions, or behaviors of others. Thus, it is a life skill no
one can afford to be without. It is an art requiring charisma to establish
trust and credibility, and a science requiring facts, information, and an
understanding of human dynamics (the purpose of this book). Persuasion
also requires highly polished communications skills that blend art and

science. Remember, you can't influence a customer, team member, or audience if you first don't know who they are. The twelve principles of influence described herein will introduce you to mental shortcuts or persuasion triggers that will provide you with a competitive edge.

Although people often confuse persuasion with negotiation, the two are distinctively different, even though both skills are often used in conflict resolution. Persuasion is done with the intention of changing attitudes, beliefs, opinions, or behavior through voluntary compliance. In persuasion, the aim is to reach a pre-determined outcome on the part of one party. In negotiation, although persuasion may be involved, the aim is to bring both parties to an agreement with the outcome often quite different from what either side thought in the beginning. In persuasion, there is not just acceptance of what you want, but also a willingness to do what you want.

While influence and persuasion are part of the negotiation process, negotiations are for the purpose of a win-win agreement by exchanging ideas with the intention of changing relationships. Negotiations are more of an intricate dance of give-and-take where influence is more interactive and reciprocal. Negotiation is more of a two-way street whereas persuasion is the ability to influence the thoughts, attitudes, and behaviors of others into compliance with your beliefs and values. While negotiations have a different intention and are directed by compromise and agreement, in *Negotiate Like the Pros*, John Patrick Dolan suggests strategies that will improve your persuasion power:

Persuasion Strategies

1. Know what you want (in vivid detail) and ask for it.
2. Confidence: Expect "Yes."
3. Know their wants and their values.
4. Preparation and information. Knowledge is power.
5. Organize your thoughts.
6. Think through what you will say, not just about what you will say.
7. Actions speak louder than words.
8. Be concise.
9. Focus on the benefits to them.
10. Listen to learn and understand facts, feelings, and between the lines.
11. Respond with questions to facilitate a clearer understanding.
12. Mentally organize their thoughts in your mind.

Charm and seduction are often omitted from discussions on influence and persuasion when, in fact, they are primary to influence. President Clinton used his charm quite well during the investigations of his affair with Monica Lewinsky. Charmers deflect attention from themselves and focus it on their target. They understand your spirit, feel your pain, and adapt to your moods. Charm is seduction without sex according to Robert Greene in *The Art of Seduction.* He contrasts charm with charisma and explains charm as an inner quality—self-confidence, sexual energy, sense of purpose, contentment—that most people lack and want. They create the aura of being extraordinary and superior as they radiate intensity while remaining detached. People are drawn to those who have already attracted attention. By doing the unexpected and creating suspense, these charmers are always one step ahead and in control.

Power: Why People Want It But Deny It

Because of the misuse and abuse of power as evidenced by coercion and corruption, many are suspicious and fearful of power. Even back in 1887, Lord Acton of Britain reflected such sentiment at that time stating, "Power tends to corrupt and, absolute power corrupts absolutely." This may explain why many people who have power deny it, and those who want it won't admit it. However, the most desirable power is personal power; it is the power you have when power by position and relationships is removed. It's an inside job. In reality, it is those who feel powerless that can be most aggressive and tyrannical, while true leadership is demonstrated by those who are confident and comfortable with the power they have. Visionary leader Dee Hock explained the heart and soul of leadership as this: "If you look to lead, invest at least 40% of your time managing yourself—your ethics, character, principles, purpose, motivation, and conduct. Invest at least 30% managing those with authority over you, and 15% managing your peers. Use the remainder to induce those you 'work for' to understand and practice [these principles]. I use the term 'work for' advisedly, for if you don't understand that you should be working for your mislabeled subordinates, you haven't understood anything."

While consistency and continuity in our messages build trust and credibility, Greene also suggests that sending mixed signals—being tough and tender, spiritual yet earthly, innocent but cunning—suggests depth and thus fascinates as it confuses. Since pain and anxiety are precursors to pleasure, tension and disharmony are necessary for you to be seen as the answer to their problems. The way to lure people out of their defensive shell is to enter their spirit by playing by their rules, enjoy what they enjoy, and adapt to their moods. (Dating often exemplifies this dance of deception, for after the honeymoon, relationships take a turn as people reveal their true selves.)

Greene explains that seducers draw you in by the focused, individualized attention they give you by aiming at universal weaknesses—vanity and self-esteem. Anti-seducers lack awareness and never realize when they are pestering, imposing, or talking too much and thus repelling others. They are insecure, self-absorbed, and forget to validate the presence of the other. There is no profit or pleasure in dealing with the anti-seducer.

In *The Psychology of Influence*, Kevin Hogan makes reference to influence and persuasion being part of human culture since the beginning of time, citing master persuaders from the Holy Bible (there were many):

> There is the well-known story in the Bible of a man who was able to convince a multitude of his fellow slaves to rise up and leave Egypt. The slaves knew, of course, that they could not succeed. It would be impossible to escape from the army of Pharaoh and, once in the desert, there would be no possibilities of survival. They had no weapons, little food, and a minimum of possessions. Knowing this, Moses told his people that God had given him instructions to go, spend forty years in the desert, then enter into the Promised Land. Moses not only had to convince the Hebrews to leave Egypt, he had to convince them that God talked to him. He then had to persuade them to believe they would survive the trek to Palestine. What would the fate for the Hebrew people have been had Moses failed to persuade those thousands that he was for real? What did Moses possess that other biblical leaders did not? After all, the people listened to Moses. In many other stories, the people all but ignored God's messengers.

Some of the world's most influential people never held a position of power such as being a king, queen, president, or even a boss at the local grocery store. Mother Teresa, Gandhi, Martin Luther King, and the founder of MADD (the mother who lost her child by a drunken driver), are examples of how influence is more about connecting and resonating with people than it is about power and authority. Robert Copper also cited the unarmed protestor in Tiananmen Square who stepped in front of the military tank that mowed him to his death. Although he was doomed to fail, his commitment and effort resonated with everyone. Give the world the best you have and the best will come back to you.

Five Stages of Effective Persuasion

- Establish the core value of a win/win philosophy and relationship which is crucial to positive persuasion.

- Develop a personal skill-set including a mastery of persuasion strategies, a knowledge of the laws of persuasion, and an understanding of nonverbal communications.

- Program your subconscious for success and be results oriented. By understanding different thinking styles, you can then align your message to the thought processes of each individual client or customer.

- Prepare. Gather information and get into a "win" mindset by getting psyched up.

- Design your script and tailor it to the needs and style of your client or audience.

Presentation is showtime. This is your time to connect and establish rapport. By implementing many of the techniques shared throughout this book, you will be able to speak so effectively that you will engage your audience or client and move them to action. The win/win results are then inevitable. In his most recent book *Have a Great Year Every Year*, Dave Yoho presents such guidelines in his EPOD Theory which has four elements to speak more effectively and engage your customers:

Energy—The degree of intensity, enthusiasm, and excitation which is displayed in the interaction between ourselves and others...

Persuasion—Persuasion deals mostly with language and verbal skills...getting people to respond to your ideas; getting the outcomes you want; getting others to buy into new methods, products, and services...

Optimism—Optimism is an attitude created by a personal decision. The subconscious mind does not know the difference between the real and the imagined...Optimism enables individuals to thrive in an otherwise negative environment, and by virtue of their optimism, become a conduit for change within and to the environment...

Discipline—Discipline levels can be measured by how frequently and effectively one approaches and completes tasks that he or she doesn't really like to do. Discipline is a commitment to a way of life.

The Best Advocates: Persuasion, Perseverance, and Patience

While control by force, fear, or coercion may bring short-term results, lasting cooperation and commitment can only be achieved through earned respect and trust. "Persuasion, perseverance and patience are the best advocates in questions depending on the will of others," according to Thomas Jefferson. This approach involves a willingness to customize and repackage the offer in such a way that the prospect accepts it by his or her own volition. The power of the right kind of influence is highly effective and usually produces a predictable, automatic response. On the other hand, trying to force a sale or an opinion upon another only leads to resistance. *Insist leads to resist.* The same is true for prospective buyers who will clutch their wallets and cling to their suspicions if they feel they are being pushed.

The world has changed. Slick selling techniques are now obsolete. Sophisticated consumers are more informed and opinionated, and less tolerant of pushy people. Today's consumers respond well to positive persuasion and "sway power" if presented with benevolence, sincerity, and honesty.

Self-interest is the chief catalyst for all buyers. As opposed to egotistical self-interest, the self-interest I am referring to has to do with the positive aspects of self-centeredness and self-gratification—the desire for personal fulfillment and happiness. This desire is at the center of every human or business interaction. It is the consideration that can make or break any sales or negotiation process. Thus, making a sale is not about selling in the sense of manipulating the will of a prospect. It's about giving the customer something he or she wants, a transaction in which the person is predisposed to saying "Yes."

The roots of our buying vulnerability are probably best explained by the science of ethology, which deals with the study of automatic behavior as activated by certain triggers. Certain things seem to trigger particular responses, even if it means reacting in totally uncharacteristic and inappropriate ways—like a mother turkey embracing her natural enemy because her "predator" speaks her language. The phenomenon is called a fixed-action pattern.

Ethologist M.W. Fox, in his study of the maternal habits of turkeys, discovered that they have a peculiar side to their maternal nature. Virtually all of their motherly nurturing is triggered by one thing—the cheep-cheep sound of their young. So much so, that if a chick doesn't cheep, the mother ignores it and sometimes even kills it. A cheeping predator could influence her behavior. Ethologists tell us that such an automatic response occurs in a wide variety of species, including human beings.

I have personally used this knowledge to my advantage in a number of situations. In getting out of potential speeding tickets, for example, I have used humor, asked favors, made confessions, used time urgency, proposed alternative solutions, employed my charisma, or used the officer's name as I responded to questions. I have even touched the officers on the arm as I explained why I was speeding. Once, when I was pulled over, I explained that I was so caught up in the *Battle Hymn of the Republic* playing on my car radio that I lost all awareness of my speed. The officer, an ex-serviceman, let me off with a warning.

Another time, not only did my persuasion skills save me from getting a ticket, I actually sold two of my books to the police officers. (This is *not* a suggestion to authors for book-selling strategies.) The common element in all of these situations was the effective use of fixed-action patterns, putting me in control of the situation and thus effectively persuading and influencing. In other words, I was able to "sell" my point of view by "buying" a piece of their minds.

In essence, the twelve principles of influence are things that trigger a fixed-action response from others. Once more, I must emphasize that none of these practices should replace basic goodness. Success will not come by abusing these principles in win-lose dealings, for the stench of a bad reputation brings ruin to all. There is no substitute for honesty and integrity in your intentions and motivation as you apply the twelve principles of influence and persuasion in the spirit of serving others.

We are all here on this earth to add value by serving others. If you have integrity, nothing else matters; if you don't have integrity, nothing else matters. With integrity, the essence of selling is "service." Although it is better to serve than obey, the ultimate in true service is to love.

Chapter One
The Principle of Language Leverage and Power Talk

When dealing with people, remember you are not dealing with creatures of logic, but with creatures of emotion, creatures bristling with prejudice and motivated by pride and vanity.
Dale Carnegie

Mark Twain understood how logic is seduced by words when he said, "Get your facts first, then you can distort them as you please." Logic, sequence of thought, and clarity are essential to influence and persuasion for a confused mind says "No." The power of words transforms lives and creates magic. Language is both an art and a science. It is how we convey a message and connect with others to influence and persuade. Our word choices and how we use words allow us to direct another's perception of reality and thus impact change. For example, Lee Iacocca got the financial support of the U.S. government by restructuring phrases for companies such as "bailout" (suggesting an incompetent organization) to "safety net" which has a more positive connotation. He framed Chrysler's problems as America's problems and the congress bought in and wrote him a very large check.

Glittering Generalities: The Power of Purr Words
In North Carolina, there is currently a huge debate in our state's legislature on whether we should have a state lottery. Since the state loses more than $300 million per year to neighboring states that do have a lottery, and the state desperately could use such funds to boost its educational system, this continues to be a hot issue. The proponents are not framing their cause correctly. It should not be sold as pro-lottery, a tough sell in the Bible Belt, but rather as pro-education. It

is how you frame something and what you focus on that gives your language leverage.

Although words are only seven percent of the communication process, they can make all the difference in making or breaking the deal. Words are rarely neutral because they reflect symbols that spark an emotional reaction in our unconscious mind and thus affect our attitudes, feelings, and behaviors. Advertisers, lawyers, politicians, and dictators have used and abused the power of the word to persuade and influence. In *Artful Persuasion,* Harry Mills discusses how Hitler used labels and name calling to evoke emotions and create an anti-Semitic sentiment. By referring to the Jews as "sludge," "sewage," and "bloodsuckers," Hitler effectively maneuvered the minds of many into deplorable behaviors. Although rooted in evil, Hitler was, unfortunately but obviously, a master manipulator.

President Bush then capitalized on the established mindset regarding Hitler's evildoings by linking Hitler's suppression of the Jews to the gassing of the Kurds by Saddam Hussein. This perception implied a fight between good and evil and, just as there was only one way to stop Hitler, it seemed apparent the same logic applied to Hussein. Mills also made reference to Aaron Delwiche's explanation of glittering generalities used to create approval and acceptance without examining evidence. It is name calling in reverse. Examples are "freedom of choice," "peace with honor," and "fiscal responsibility." Take a moment and think about what each one of those phrases really means. They're vague by design. According to Delwiche, a propaganda analyst, glittering generalities are "purr words" with a positive association but are ambiguous and purposely vague. Mills also cited examples of how we use bland words to take the sting out of the reality and to reduce its emotional impact. For example, calling the MX missile the "Peacekeeper" and civilian casualties just "collateral damage" seems a bit deceptive. We have altered our description of the serious emotional repercussions of fighting in a war from "shell shock" to "combat fatigue" to "post-traumatic stress disorder" which truly distances one from any direct battle scars.

Words are continually reworked to convey a more flattering image or acceptable meaning. I recently spoke for the IAAP (International Association of Administrative Professionals). Years ago I had spoken for the same group under a different name of PSI (Professional Secretaries

International). The word "secretary" has slowly become obsolete along with "beautician" and "janitor." Words obviously do count or we would not continually change them and modify their reference.

The Antitheses: End on a Positive Note

Study the structure of the speeches of great orators to discover the magic of words and how they are sequenced. In *Artful Persuasion,* Mills compares the quotes of various presidents and their use of the clever rhetorical device called antithesis such as "When the going gets tough, the tough get going." President Kennedy's may be the most quoted antithesis, "Ask not what your country can do for you—but what you can do for your country." The reason Ronald Reagan, often called the great communicator, is so rarely quoted in comparison to Kennedy is due to how their writers used the antithesis. While Kennedy's quotes end with a positive declaration, Reagan's quotes often end with the negative side of the antithesis. Reverse Reagan's quote, "The future is best decided by ballots, not bullets" to "The future is decided best not by bullets, but by ballots" and you will sense the difference. The three rules for effective use of the antitheses are to keep them short and simple, have balance, and end on a positive note.

Repetition, often referred to as the "broken record," creates a hypnotic effect that cuts to the core. Will anyone ever forget Lincoln's famous use of repetition with, "government of the people, by the people, for the people?" Martin Luther King also moved the masses with his repetition of "I have a dream."

The most powerful word you can use is another's name—especially the one with which they are most identified (which is often their first name). If you can get permission to use their first name, use it! People are receptive to the familiar and everyone is familiar with their own name. While the formality of using their last name may be appropriate, it can also be a distancing factor in the relationship and actually work against you.

"Please" and "thank you" are the next most important words as they show respect and gratitude. "Because" follows as the next most powerful word as logic and reason give understanding to a request, thus people tend to comply.

For example, Ellen Langer, a Harvard social psychologist, did a study in 1977 where she approached people waiting to use the copier with, "Excuse me, I have five pages," and 60% allowed her move ahead.

When she simply added these words, "Excuse me, I have five pages. May I use the machine because I am in a rush," she found 94% allowed her to move ahead of them. When I am running late for a flight, using "because" has prevented me from many a travel disaster. (Leaving a bit earlier would also prevent missing those flights.) Since that study was done almost thirty years ago, I am not sure people would be quite as obliging today as they were back in the 1970s. After all, that was soon after the love children had planted their seeds of kindness on the earth.

Framing: It's How You Say It

It is not only the words we use, but also how we sequence and frame them that determines the response we get. A story that illustrates the importance of framing is that of two priests who were heavy smokers but were denied their deadly pleasure while praying (which was most of their day). Hoping to change the rules, they each had approached the bishop to get permission to smoke while they prayed. The first priest was punished for even asking if he might smoke while he prayed. However, the second priest was not only given permission, but was applauded for his honor after simply asking, "May I pray while I smoke."

Your choice of words will either add strength to your message or weaken it. Get rid of the "ifs," "ands," and "buts" that convey doubt. No one ever put confidence in those who first did not believe in themselves. Use affirmative language, speak with conviction, and be decisive to convey confidence and credibility. Hedge words and qualifiers such as "sort of," or "kind of," and "maybe" convey insecurity. People of power do not sit on the fence.

While it is appropriate to apologize, over-politeness communicates timidity or poor self-esteem. Never introduce yourself with disclaimers of what and who you are not. Many high-powered CEOs begin their presentations with apologies of being a lousy speaker. Starting their talk in such a manner speaks for itself. These folks don't have to affirm their obvious weakness. Most certainly, it is better to begin a discussion or presentation on a positive note.

What detracts from your persuasive power are "fillers" such as "uh" or "umm." Tag questions such as "Don't you think," after a statement conveys uncertainty. "It's a nice day, don't you think?" communicates that you can't even decide if the day is nice or not. Intensifiers such as "very" actually diminish the power of your statement. Saying "It is lovely" puts the emphasis on lovely where it belongs rather than saying "It is so very, very, very lovely." Guess what. Lovely gets lost.

Let your integrity speak for itself. My dad always prefaced his statements with "To tell the truth," or "To be perfectly honest." It was one lesson I wish I had not learned, for to advertise that you are telling the truth creates questions on what might have been a lie.

High Energy Words Move People to Action

In his *Power Linguistics* program, Dave Yoho emphasizes the suppression of first-person reference or "I" and suggests using more "you" and "your." The focus must not be on what you have but what the prospect needs. How you use your language and your positive energy level directly increases your ability to persuade. There are words and phrases that emit low energy and are de-persuasive as opposed to words that emit high energy and thus influence people and move them to action. Overused clichés and meaningless adjectives neutralize and can be annoying. The following is a list of words Yoho suggests that you avoid:

Words to Avoid

Fabulous	I – we – me
Brand-new	Out of this world
Unbelievable	Like…like…like
To tell the truth	Between you and me
Do you follow me?	How are you today?
You know…	What's up?
May I help you?	You should, ought, or must

Advertisers refer to the "hook," which is the use of words to grab attention and gently lure people to listen or to read on and then hopefully take action. Emotional words often used include the following:

Free	Exciting	Vital	Easy
Save	Love	Proud	Benefit
Money	Safety	Truth	Instant
Profit	Joy	Fun	Deserve
Proven	Desire	Improved	Right
Guarantee	Value	New	Advantage
Powerful	Integrity	Health	Investment

As a hypnotherapist and psychotherapist, I have always been in the role of influencing and persuading people to quit smoking, lose weight, reduce their anxieties, or shift from depression to joy. Since I am not a medical doctor and cannot prescribe drugs, words are my magic. Understanding language patterns are crucial for change whether you are selling a product or encouraging people to achieve their personal and professional goals.

For example, the unconscious mind cannot distinguish between a "do" and a "do not" message. Also, people cannot make a picture of the word "don't" in their minds because it is not a noun. Therefore, when we say "don't" and then follow it with a guiding suggestion, the receiver only hears the suggestion for action. An example is, "Don't decide now. Just call me when you decide that you will want to move forward with the program." Another suggestive statement would be, "I don't know if reading this book will increase your sales and your ability to influence and persuade others." (You just programmed their mind with the suggestion that as they read this book, their ability to influence and persuade others is being increased.)

A few other suggestions on how to use persuasive language and how to apply some principles of Neuro-Linguistic Programming (NLP) include using the words "might" and "maybe" to gently nudge someone into action rather than demand that action, which often creates resistance. An example is, "Maybe you will want to surprise me with a special gift," or "You might notice how your energy level increases right after taking the supplement."

Resistance-Proof Language

Another effective language pattern is to assume your client knows something they really don't have a clue about. The assumed knowledge word or phrase can be very convincing. Think of how you can gently move someone along by saying, "You probably already know you will buy it," or "Eventually, you will realize this is the best decision you have ever made." Now that's planting seeds of persuasion!

It is also important that you present controversial issues in a language that is resistance proof. By saying, "I could tell you that you are making a mistake, but I won't. You want to figure that out for yourself." Even if you put it in the negative, the effect will be just as persuasive such as, "I wouldn't tell you to leave your job because you need to come to that conclusion yourself."

Once again, by getting people in the pattern of answering "Yes," either verbally or internally, you are getting them into an open and receptive mind state. After being in agreement with so many of your questions and sharing a common truth, it is counter-intuitive to suddenly switch to "No" or a position of disagreement.

Two other ways to gain language leverage is *future pacing* where their decision to buy commits them to future sales. Here is a question you might ask to make that suggestion. "If you are pleased with our service, will you let us take care of your regional needs as well?" Remember, one of the principles of influence and persuasion is that of commitment and consistency. Don't be blind to opportunities that are staring you in the face.

While much of one's credibility is associated with physical presentation of self and style, words can also add or detract from credibility statements and must never exaggerate or tell people something is more than they can possibly believe. Pointing out negative aspects of a product or service can be disarming and increases trust. It makes you appear objective, and by you pointing out the negatives, they can then focus on the benefits. When you pull back, they will push forward with nothing to resist.

Objections are a sign that a decision is being processed and is being seriously considered. How you deal with objections can actually increase trust.

Responding to Objections

- Clarify the concern. Restate and paraphrase the objection to assure you understand it.
- Welcome and encourage their objection. Rather than avoid or run from it, move into it to create a sense of alignment
- Listen to understand and then acknowledge and affirm.
- Present proof through testimonials and examples in a calm, confident manner. Confirm that their concerns are resolved and get their feedback.
- Diffusion: Present the positive side of the negative. For example, if the price is a concern, indicate how that may reflect higher quality and reliability; then focus on value.

Metaphors: Persuasion Power through Images

Speaking in metaphors is the most powerful persuader of all the language skills. A metaphor is an imaginative way of describing something by saying it is something else. It is a more concrete, personal, and image-provoking way to create vivid messages that linger and last. Metaphors frame the way we think. Like a window frame, metaphors limit what we can see and thus focus us on certain things while obscuring other features and, therefore, change attitudes.

Martin Luther King was a master of the metaphor. In his "I Have a Dream" speech in 1963, King's words moved mountains. "I have a dream...that the sons of former slaves and the sons of former slave owners will be able to sit down together at the table of brotherhood; that one day, even the state of Mississippi, a state sweltering with the heat of injustice, sweltering with the heat of oppression, will be transformed into an oasis of freedom and justice."

The Domino Theory is a metaphor that was used by President Dwight Eisenhower and Secretary of State John Foster Dulles to portray the threat and spread of communism. The theory was based on a fear that if one country fell to the communists, the others would also fall, one after the other "like a row of dominoes." Lyndon B. Johnson bought into the metaphor and thus 58,000 troops were lost in our support of South Vietnam.

While language and words are lodged in the left-brain along with our logical thinking, language and our words ignite emotions. Mike Hughes, the President of Market-Ability, reveals that John Caples changed the word "repair" to the word "fix" and saw a 20% increase in response. We buy what we want and then seek to justify it with why we might "need" it. Language must be vivid to ignite emotions—the single most powerful force of persuasion. People may be persuaded by reason, but they are moved to action by emotion. Emotions, not logic, provide a shortcut to behavioral change and can create instant influence.

An emotional pitch takes a lot less cognitive effort than weighing all the pros and cons and is much more interesting, especially if it creates pictures and uses music. Emotional arguments disarm people and gently nudge them to drop their defenses. Besides, people are not influenced often by facts, but rather what makes the most vivid impression on their minds. For example, when *Jaws* opened at cinemas across the United States, the number of swimmers visiting California beaches dramatically decreased. The fact is that, although sharks inhabit the California coast, the risk of a swimmer actually being attacked by a shark is much less than the risk of being killed in a car accident while driving to the beach.

The Language of Truth

Another area where language takes a back seat is in gender differences. In her book *Why So Slow?*, psychologist and educator Virginia Valian reveals that gender in the lives of men and women rather than their speech make the big difference in how they are perceived. In her studies, she arrived at the following conclusions:

- *Women internalize failure more than men.*
- *Women are less influential than men in a group decision.*
- *Attractiveness has a negative impact on the perception of a woman's competence and a positive impact on the perception of a man's competence.*
- *Both men and women elicit a negative response when they are assertive or try to solve a problem, but women are judged more negatively than men.*
- *Women's successes are more likely to be attributed to luck than to skill; men's successes are more likely to be attributed to skill than to luck.*
- *Women expect to receive fewer benefits from their work than men do.*
- *Women often overestimate the difficulty of a task; men often underestimate the difficulty of a task.*
- *Women, when they talk, are attended to less than men by both men and women.*

There certainly are other factors and variables such as rank, authority, and position. Janet Reno and Madeleine Albright were heard in spite of being women. However, although both were very intelligent and respected women, attractiveness was not their greatest strength which endorses Valian's conclusions. Minds tend to be limited by either/or thinking and need to expand to the consciousness that attractive women can have functional brains too.

We also must be observant of how language and communications can be blamed for deeper conflicts and issues. For example, "You're not listening to me," may really mean, "You're not doing what I want you to do."

Words can also be used to be polite, meaning that people use words to tell little white lies which is the use of words to protect the harshness of the truth—people lie. If you are in sales, how many times have you heard the sweet refrains of, "I'm just looking; I'll get back to you on that; I need to think it over; I need to check it out with my husband or wife." (And you're not even married.) Yes, words do have power but your body doesn't lie which is why Chapter Three is devoted to the language of truth.

In *Power Talk*, Sarah Myers McGinty introduces the concept of language from the center as opposed to language from the edge.

Language From The Center
- *Directs Rather Than Responds*
- *Makes Statements*
- *Contextualizes with Authority*
- *Contradicts, Argues, and Disagrees*
- *Practices Affect of Control*

Dr. Myers explains how language from the center reflects qualities of leadership such as competence, knowledge, and authority. In contrast, she lists how language from the edge sounds different.

Language From The Edge
- *Responds Rather Than Directs*
- *Asks Questions*
- *Contextualizes with Protective Strategies*
- *Avoids Open Argument*
- *Practices Conversational Maintenance*

Language from the edge conveys more approachability, inclusion, inquiry, and caution. Since persuasion is based on our language and communications skills, it is important that we become more conscious of how we speak. Myers also provides a model for self-observation to increase awareness.

- Looking In
- Looking Out
- Trying In
- Trying Out

Myers describes *looking in* as studying your own conversations to determine how you sound, how much you say, how long you talk, and how many questions you may ask. She describes *looking out* as being aware of adopting the vernacular of the culture such as their vocabulary and their jargon. *Trying in* is testing the feasibility of a new behavior or speech tactic, while Myers defines *trying out* as testing your new behavior in a more public setting. While awareness will give you increased control, the fact is that your speech is as individual as a fingerprint and thus you will always prefer your core style because language and speech habits are intimate with identity. She cites the controversy over the recognition of Black Vernacular English or Ebonics and the Québécois in Canada as examples of how tempers flare when our language or use of it is challenged. This emotional bond or bondage to our language can make us relatively unconscious of our communication style that lends to inflexibility and a lack of control. This can be an obstacle that must be overcome for you to be more influential, for the power of persuasion is most effective when we first bond with another and connect by speaking "their" language.

As we speak another's language, Donald Moine and Kenneth Lloyd explain in *Unlimited Selling Power* how some words can actually "freeze" a customer's thinking. Using "Frozen Words" you can take processes (such as thinking or emotions) and turn them into fixed events (such as decisions). Their example was that if a customer would say his thinking was that he was not ready to buy the product just yet, you would ask what his thought might be as to when he would be ready to decide to buy. As a psychotherapist I have personally used the same process by turning constantly changing feelings into a concrete thing. For example, if someone said they were feeling scared and insecure, I would simply ask them what would enable them to feel confident instead. It is basically forwarding and directing the customer's thinking process into a tangible thing they can possess and own such as confidence.

You can also "unfreeze" a customer's decision not to buy. By taking a process such as decision-making that has been turned into a fixed hard thing—a decision, you can then turn it back into a fluid process of deciding. While a decision is hard to change, "deciding" is an on-going process and thus you can unfreeze your customer's thinking to make a better choice—as you would define it.

Vague verbs leaves the details up to your client's imagination which not only triggers their active participation, but allows them to sell themselves, for the details they supply are more meaningful than what you may provide. Besides, by encouraging them to customize your vague sales presentation, their imagination will have no limitations and neither will your sales.

Comparative words effortlessly get the customer to make comparisons such as faster, better, lighter, or stronger, and also build trust and a climate of agreement. Once that trust is established, the power of absolutes reflects not only your confidence but also your confidence in the product. A true sales superstar also knows how to take the power out of absolute words when a customer objects. For example, if a customer states she would never buy a foreign product, with some exaggeration, you might simply ask, "Never?" When you hear such absolutes such as "never," "always," or "nothing," look for the exception by asking, "Has there ever been an exception to that rule?"

Superwords or superlatives such as "fastest," or "strongest," "most," or "least," must be used only when in truth it really is. Again, leaving out the information that specifies why or how a product or service is the best allows the customer to project his own beliefs based on his wants and needs. Master salespeople also will literally make their products talk or give them other human qualities which is unthreatening and creates a lasting memory and impression.

Sales Superstars also continually renew and refine their sales script book. Learn to anticipate all questions, stalls, objections, and resistances. The best learning strategy to observe and integrate the sales styles of top performers in action.

In *The Success Principles,* Jack Canfield sites Don Miguel Ruiz's insights on speaking with impeccability in his book, *The Four Agreements.* When you speak with impeccability, your words have power not only with yourself but also with others for these words are the basis of all relationships. Thus successful people are masters of the "word," and speak words of inclusion rather than words of separation, words of acceptance rather than words of rejection, and words of tolerance rather than words of prejudice. They are conscious of the thoughts they think and the words they speak which always build self-esteem, confidence, relationships, dreams, love, possibilities, and vision. Your words put out an energy and message that creates a reaction in others that is usually returned to you multiplied. Everything you say produces an effect in the world, and thus you are always creating something—either positive or negative—with your words which should be impeccable. Unfortunately no one ever taught us how powerful words can be. Canfield sites Ruiz in the following suggestion on speaking with impeccability.

Addressing Others with Impeccability

- Make a commitment to be impeccable in your speech when talking to others.
- Make an effort to appreciate something about every person you interact with.
- Make a commitment to tell the truth, as best you can in all of your interactions and dealing with others. Make a commitment to do it for one day, then two days in a row, then a whole week. If you falter, start over. Keep building that muscle.
- Make it the intention of every interaction with others that you uplift them in some small way. Notice how you feel when you do that.

To speak with impeccability is to speak from your highest self with intention and integrity. It means that your words are in alignment with your dreams and visions of success. However, the most powerful words are often those not spoken.

Silence Is Golden: It's Also Power

Silence is a universal language of power. It's a bit of the "next person who speaks loses" syndrome according to John Patrick Dolan. Remember, he who speaks first comes in last. Just let the silence do the talking for you. Most people can't stand dead airtime and if you can, you have the control.

Over twenty years ago, I was almost blown off my chair when my accountant presented an astronomical bill of over $2,000.00 just to do my personal taxes. Now, organization is not my strength, but come on, two grand way back in 1980, when gas was 49 cents a gallon, seemed a bit steep. Being totally numb, I said absolutely nothing waiting for him to say something like, "April Fool!" Instead, he said, "$1,700.00." Still trying to come out of my coma, I remained silent and heard "$1,500.00." While numbers and math petrify me, I do observe patterns well and realized I was on to something—the power of silence.

It got better. I then heard "$1,400.00" and noticed the decrements were decreasing, but the trend continued as he then offered "$1, 250.00." At this point, my power was embarrassing me and felt that, to be fair, I needed to accept the offer and did agree.

Silence *is* golden and also a powerful persuader.

Persuasion Tactics

- Frame your message. Use words in a sequence and context that will positively frame and focus your message. Use your words to lead people to where you want them to go.

- Choose words that evoke emotions, for without emotion there is no motion.

- Make your statements memorable. Keep your message short and simple, and make sure it has balance and ends on a positive note.

- Repetition is the laser of language and gives you the upper edge by cutting to the core.

- Get rid of disengaging words such as "I," fillers, tag words, hedge words, and intensifiers which all diminish your message.

- Plant seeds of positive suggestion even in your negative statements. Suggest that their decision to buy now commits them to future transactions. Influence is an ongoing process. You don't plant for just one harvest but for a life of prosperity.

- State their objections before they even notice them. Control objections by introducing them. It builds trust.

- Become a Diva of Diffusion. Learn to present the positive of every negative.

- Speak "their" language. Mirror what they do, match how they think and talk because words symbolize thoughts and language redirects thinking.

Chapter Two
The Principle of Resonance
and the Silent Sell

The more you can effectively interpret body language, the more influential and persuasive you will become. We respond to gestures with an extreme alertness and, one might almost say, in accordance with an elaborate and secret code that is written nowhere, known by none, and understood by all.
F. Sapir

Master persuaders resonate and build immediate rapport with others and create an emotional mind share. In little or no time, people feel comfortable around them and instant trust, compatibility, and emotional bonding is established. Such resonation is often confused with love at first sight, which is a whole other book. According to Kurt Mortensen, the author of *Maximum Influence,* "The more we connect and bond with people, the more persuasive we become. We like people who are similar to us…this holds true in areas of opinions, personality traits, background, and lifestyle."

He Who Bonds—Buys
Rapport and these emotional connections are so powerful they cause us to suspend reason and ignore, distort, or minimize contrary evidence. It is the "rose-colored glasses" syndrome. The main work of a trial attorney is to make a jury "like his client," according to Clarence Darrow. Any sensible lawyer knows that if jurors feel they share some common ground with a defendant—and better yet, grow to *like* that person—then he or she has a markedly better chance of an acquittal. That's the chief reason why we are so surprised at some of the verdicts we hear. A persuasive lawyer such as Johnnie Cochrane was able to

create a rapport between the jury and his client and also direct their attention and focus to the case being a racial issue rather than murder.

Establishing rapport is the central focus in Neuro-Linguistic Programming (NLP), which is a powerful communication system that creates immediate rapport and behavioral change. Dale Carnegie's classic, *How to Win Friends and Influence People*, cites studies that show as much as 90 percent of our success depends on our people skills; specifically, on our ability to get others to like us. Although important, technical skills, product quality, and service distinction will not keep customers loyal if we don't score high on people skills. How do you rate a hospital, an airline, or a restaurant? With experienced surgeons, the best trained pilots, and a world premiere chef, if the nursing assistant, the attendant, and the waitress are not resonating well with you, the quality behind the scenes is irrelevant. The more high tech the world becomes, the more high touch and relationships are the deciding factors in all transactions. You need to sell yourself before you can sell your product, service, or opinion. He who bonds—buys.

Tupperware, Amway, and Pampered Chef home parties exercise the strength of the social bonding which exerts tremendous pressure on friends buying from friends. It is the unwritten rule woven with expectations and social consensus. The powers of persuasion are similarity and familiarity, so the foundation is already in place at such parties.

Masters of sway use familiarity and similarity to build rapport and increase their likeability by finding, and even exaggerating, common interests. Car salespeople, for example, are trained to look for evidence of commonalities when a prospect shows up with a trade-in. If there is camping gear in the vehicle, the salesperson might mention how he or she loves to go hiking and camping (only to sometimes find out it's their neighbor's gear and that they detest the activity). If there are golf clubs, the savvy salesperson may remark that he or she plans to play eighteen holes later that week. A child seat in the back is an opening to talk about the salesperson's own children and the importance of child safety. These similarities may be truthful, exaggerated similarities, or even lies (which I do not recommend), but the ensuing exchange helps to establish rapport and moves the sales/prospect relationship to a more intimate buddy-buddy dimension. Sales literature is filled with stories about those who made a fortune by virtue of relationship selling. Relationship selling is not going away anytime soon.

Open Emotional Bank Accounts

One of the leaders in the field, Joe Girard, specializes in emotional mind sharing. He has sold millions of dollars worth of Chevrolets, winning the title "Number One Car Salesman in America" for twelve years straight. He averaged over five cars and trucks sold for every day he worked. Joe has a spot in the *Guinness Book of World Records* as the world's greatest car salesman. He willingly shares the very simple secret of his phenomenal success: "Offer people a fair price from someone they like to buy from, and you can sell a lot of cars." Joe opened emotional bank accounts with his customers and makes unlimited deposits into these accounts every chance he gets. He used the currency of smiles, compliments, shared interests, humor, care and concern, kindness, interesting tidbits of information, and hospitality to build immediate rapport and likeability.

One of the quickest ways he forms immediate bonds is remembering and using customers' names. It is one of many tactics that all of the masters of sway use to develop rapport and exert influence, converting prospects into customers. The most effective leaders and managers do the same thing when they need to build strong cohesive work teams. Believe it or not, it also works for parents when they address their children by their full birth name if they need compliance or cooperation.

Researchers have found that if you use a person's name at both the beginning and end of sentences, your "swayability" dramatically increases because it triggers an immediate bond. Although a simple strategy, it is effective because it connects with the emotional brain, which is excited by the familiar, and thus converts resistance into cooperation. Remembering someone's name is a function of listening and not a function of memory. When someone tells you his or her name, pronounce it several times to yourself or out loud. Clarify the spelling and associate their name with something familiar. An example would be if you meet Molly and she has an alluring mole. You then make "mole" a trigger to remember her name such as "Molly with the mole."

Master persuaders use just the right amount of common values, beliefs, interests, and background similarities to create an "emotional cocktail" that wins the prospect over. Bundling a prospect's name into your sales pitch is an important ingredient in that cocktail. People are emotionally attached to their names which are, after all, part of their identity. When you top off the mix of product, price, and likeability with the person's name, it becomes delightfully intoxicating.

A marketing mandate is to generate more mind share by bonding with prospects and once the relationship is established, give them permission to sell themselves and buy your products and services because *they want to*. In his enlightening book *Working With Emotional Intelligence*, Daniel Goleman describes the role both business people and leaders must play in our world today: "The rules for work are changing. We're being judged by a new yardstick; not just by how smart we are, or by our training and expertise, but also by how well we handle ourselves and establish emotional connections with others." Marc Gobé, CEO of a top brand image creation firm, puts it another way, "The biggest misconception in sales strategies is the belief that branding is about market share when it is really about 'mind and emotions share.'" Emotional mind share paves the way to future profits.

Emotional mind share turns a selling event into a long-term relationship. Howard Shultz, CEO of Starbucks, speaks about romancing the customer. "If we greet customers, exchange a few extra words with them, then custom-make a drink exactly to their taste, we have created a friendly buying experience they will want to repeat." George Merck, one of the founders of the highly successful pharmaceutical company, agrees with Howard Schultz. "Do good and good will follow. Help your customers and you'll never fail to make a profit." Unlike Starbucks and Merck, many companies are alarmingly out of touch from the current changes in customers' buying habits and expectations.

Truly effective leaders in any industry are masters of gaining emotional mind share. They know that true empowerment, the emotional kind, grows out of cultivating solid relationships more than it does out of efficiency programs, laminated mission statements, or committees. The old managerial roles of cop and captain are giving way to coach and counselor. The sustaining power behind a more "employee friendly" workplace will come from leaders who realize they are in the relationship business.

Your Body Is Your Visual Resumé

Communications is the core of all relationships and since verbal communications makes up a meager seven percent of communications, our nonverbal communications or body language is the driving force behind the more subtle silent sell. Whether we realize it or not, we are constantly reading and being read by others. You cannot *not* communicate. Without even saying a word, we reveal a considerable amount of information about ourselves through our body language. Everything about us, no matter how slight or subtle, communicates something to someone. More is actually communicated by what we don't say. In fact, 93 percent of the messages we send to others come from our gestures, facial expressions, tone of voice, breathing, and eye contact.

This means that both you and your prospect are in the "body business." When you can read body language, you can see the receptivity or defensiveness or tension in others. You sense rejection and suspicion. You can identify the emotions, level of confidence, shyness, and mood of others. You judge others and are judged by the way you act and look. Others make decisions about what kind of person you are, your skills and competencies, your attitude and intellect, your credibility and professionalism. True, we say that inner beauty is what really counts, that we should not judge others by external appearances, but in reality, physical attractiveness and appearance play significant roles in how we size up each other. Your body is your visual resumé. When you enter a room, meet a prospect, dine at a restaurant, go into a bank, your body speaks and instant impressions are made.

The masters of sway recognize this and pay particular attention to their appearance, and how they speak and act. Think of how you respond to someone who is slouched as opposed to someone who conveys presence by their upright posture. This last point is illustrated by a story worth repeating here. About a hundred years ago in Berlin, Herr von Osten had a horse called Clever Hans. Von Osten taught Hans how to count by tapping his front hoof. Hans was a quick learner and soon progressed from simple addition to multiplication, division, and subtraction. Von Osten began touring with his horse. Clever Hans could count the number of people in the audience, the number wearing hats or glasses, the number of men versus women and children. He could tell time, use a calendar, recall musical pitch, and perform many other feats. After von Osten taught the horse to tap out the alphabet with his hoof, Hans learned to answer written questions as well. For a year and a half, the clever horse baffled audiences all across Germany. It seemed that this common, ordinary horse had intelligence beyond that of many human beings. It understood the German language and could produce the equivalent of words and numbers.

Actually, Hans' success was the result of his ability to read body language. Onlookers would relax and tilt their heads slightly when he got to the right answer, which became Hans' clue to stop tapping. Hans' cleverness was in his ability to observe the almost imperceptible and unconscious movements on the part of his trainer and the audience. He understood the relationship between a relaxed posture, head nods, his owner's tension, and the correct answer. Clearly, human beings who can correctly interpret body language are positioned to influence, persuade, and succeed.

Your Body Doesn't Lie

Let's consider some parts of the body that can increase our effectiveness at persuasion, beginning with the eyes. You have no doubt heard expressions such as, "The eyes are the windows to the soul," "We're seeing eye to eye," "The evil eye," "If looks could kill..." People pay close attention to the eyes which reveal the inner world of the other. When one of our most charismatic presidents Bill Clinton vehemently confirmed, "I did not have sex with that woman," his eyes were blinking like a flashing red light and he was unable to maintain his usual powerful eye contact with the American people. Let's face it—your body doesn't lie. You can't stop sweating. If you have gotten an icy stare, you know what I'm talking about. Eyes can scream at you when they communicate anger or disapproval. We refer to "smiling eyes" when pleased and happy with another's actions. When it comes to communicating persuasiveness, wandering eyes can sour a deal. How many times have you talked to someone at a networking event who is always looking elsewhere and scanning the room for better opportunities? Public speakers whose eyes are glued to their notes lose their connection with the audience, if they ever even established one. Wandering eyes can undermine your credibility, puncturing your persuasiveness. Salespeople need eye contact to gauge the buyer's interest or disinterest. Eye contact fuels the intimacy and warmth in a romantic relationship.

We tend to make more eye contact with people we like, people we consider higher status than us, and people we are attracted to romantically. Masters of sway position themselves to manage "eye choreography" for maximum persuasiveness. In fact, one of the skills they have is working knowledge of NLP. Richard Bandler and John Grinder, the creators of NLP, use their expertise in linguistics, psychology, and cybernetics to explain how choosing the right words and assessing eye patterns help build rapport and determine the best way to influence the sale. Eye-power can be one of the most useful tools in your sales kit.

Besides the eyes, the face itself has an incredible communication role. Communications researchers believe we can make and recognize almost 250,000 distinct facial expressions. Our face is ever so transparent as we unknowingly give ourselves away. You will no doubt recognize the following expressions which will reveal how revealing the face can be: "It's as plain as the nose on your face." "She cut off her nose to spite her face." "He's got his game face on." "If you're enjoying yourself so much, why don't you tell your face?"

Smiles: The Cornerstone of Emotional Mind Share

Smile, and the world smiles with you. Frown, and you frown alone. A smile lights up a room, for it signals warmth, happiness, joy, which is difficult not to return.

A simple thing like curving your mouth into a smile can make a significant difference, for smiles can save you miles of rhetoric when you are pitching your product or service. In fact, people can actually "hear" you smile over the phone, which I am sure you have experienced. Smiles lighten the voice and add a sense of groundedness and ease and trust to conversation. They are infectious communication devices. Smiles will help you get and keep customers, attract friends and deepen relationships, build rapport with colleagues, and smooth the rough edges in life. They are one of the cornerstones for emotional mind share.

Consider the handshake. What is your response to a loose, limp handshake? They should be firm and enthusiastic, not crushing, not jack-hammer-like. Handshakes can communicate warmth, confidence, and interest. Combined with appropriate eye contact and an infectious smile, handshakes make for a powerful first impression. In the initial contact, a potential client or customer may feel more open or closed to you just on the basis of these three considerations.

Touch is a "touchy" issue, but it can be highly effective as well. It can be delicate because, if we have negative associations with touch such as being physically disciplined or restrained, or dislike a relative stranger getting too familiar too fast, touching becomes an aggressive act and intrusion. On the other hand, if we associate touch with warmth, love, and positive experiences, we then like to be touched and we are perceived as approachable and likeable. A master at the art of influence is attuned to people's touchability and responses.

Touching someone appropriately can help put that person at ease, making him or her more receptive to you. Waiters and waitresses who touched customers on the arm when asking if everything was okay received larger tips. Librarians improved their ratings when they subtlely touched people as they handed them the books. As mentioned before, one of the techniques I used to persuade police to not give me a speeding ticket was a touch on the arm while explaining my hurry. It has never failed me.

Where you touch someone—whether it's a customer, colleague or subordinate—depends on the situation and the relationship you've established. Safe areas of contact are the shoulders, upper arms, forearms, and hands. Touching is situational and thus the masters of persuasion know when and how to use it for maximum impact.

Gestures are an important part of effective communications for influencing others. Understanding body language and how to use mirroring to gain rapport are essential tools in the art of influence and the following are guidelines for more effective use of body language:

Guidelines for Body Language

- Lean closer toward your customer to show your interest and comfort. Leaning away or fidgeting shows lack of interest or impatience.
- Refrain from covering your mouth with your fingers or hands. It signals lack of confidence or deception.
- Nodding shows interest, agreement, and understanding. It is an excellent gesture to assure others that they have your full attention.
- When you tilt your head slightly to the side during conversation, it usually conveys your interest and attention.
- Although stooped shoulders and bowed heads can mean different things, they're usually interpreted negatively, so it is better to keep your back straight and head upright. Erect posture conveys alertness, confidence, and a powerful presence.
- Stand facing the person squarely with both feet firmly planted and shoulder width apart.

- Avoid shifting weight too often. It gives the impression you are tired or uneasy.

NLP holds that we each have a primary sensory preference—visual, auditory, or kinesthetic. Anxiety, joy, tension, and sadness all have facial and bodily responses that telegraph our emotional state and personal sensory preference. We often reveal our preference in the way we speak. For instance, a person with a visual preference might ask, "Can you see what I'm saying? Do I have to draw you a picture?" Auditory people reveal themselves with references such as, "It's music to my ears; that rings a bell." The kinesthetic person is likely to say, "Let's keep in touch? I sense; I feel..." A person's use of predicates reveals their dominant sensory preference for taking in and processing information. Visual people prefer to read a brochure and look at the physical product or a picture. Auditory people want to hear about the product's features. The kinesthetic person wants to try out the product and get a feel for it. With each of these types of people, the best way to influence them is to mirror their preference, conveying the essence that you are one of them or of like kind. Birds of a feather do flock together. People also like people like themselves as it creates the commonality which is the root of all bonding—not just with those flying feathered friends. Closely observe the customer's sensory preference, then mirror and match it with your words, your body language, your dress, your energy, voice volume, your pacing or tempo, your interests, and your references. In speaking their language, the magic of rapport allows you to then lead them into your chosen direction and they will follow.

NLP is one of the most powerful communication systems I have used in my psychotherapy and coaching practice and also as a speaker and trainer. In establishing the initial rapport through the use of metaphors and stories, suggestions can then be made to change thought patterns and perceptions to initiate behavioral change.

Whether increasing your child's self-esteem and academic performance or settling a dispute between neighbors; whether selling a house or creating a high performance work team, NLP is a system that creates compliance, agreement, and cooperation.

Persuasion Tactics

- Take a good look at yourself in the mirror. What does your visual resume reveal? What do you want it to say and what changes are needed to make that happen?

- Use the enticing power of mirroring the other person's nonverbal behavior. When a prospect leans slightly toward you during your conversation, lean toward him or her. If your manager puts his hands in his pocket or crosses his arms in front of him, do likewise. When your spouse or significant other touches you, respond accordingly. Mirroring the nonverbal language of another puts you in subliminal harmony with the person. It also helps if you mirror the pacing of their speech and their energy level.

- Cross off crossing your legs and arms and causing your customers to cross theirs. In a study of over 2,500 sales people, Nierenberg and Calers found that those who had arms and legs crossed never made a sale.

- To create a powerful gesture range, practice your body movements so that you exude warmth, positive feelings, confidence, strength, and interest. Don't become mechanical, robotic, or overly theatrical. The intent is for your physiology to match your emotions and theirs.

Chapter Three
The Principle of Sensory Selling
and Alignment

I know you believe you understand what you think I said, but I am not sure you realize that what you heard is not what I meant.
Anonymous

Selling is no longer selling, but rather it is buying a piece of the customer's mind. The three strongest motivators of the buying public are as follows and in this order:

1. Fear
2. Greed
3. Exclusivity

Communication Itself Is the Communication Problem

The writings of Al Ries and Jack Trout in *Positioning: The Battle for Your Mind* have revolutionized traditional sales and marketing. They emphasize that in today's communication jungle, minds have become defensive. That observation was made before computers, email, and SPAM. Because minds are simple, in a sense, they screen and reject information due to an information overload. The mind only accepts that which matches prior knowledge or experience. Their premise is that minds don't change but instead insist, "Don't confuse me with the facts, my mind's already made up." Therefore, communication itself is the communication problem. To influence and persuade you must select the material that has the best chance of getting through. Therefore, it is crucial to focus efforts on the perceptions of the prospect rather than the reality of the product. By turning things inside out and looking for the solution to your problem inside the prospect's mind, truth surfaces.

The 22 Immutable Laws of Marketing, also by Ries and Trout, present a few laws pertinent to influence and persuasion. For example, the Law of Leadership states that it is better to be first than it is to be better. In sales, if you are first and foremost in the customer's mind, you have squatter's rights and have deep roots. People perceive the first product in their mind as superior. It's all about perception, not products. Check out your perception with the following mind-teasing questions:

What's the name of the first person to fly the Atlantic Ocean solo?
What's the name of the second person to fly the Atlantic Ocean solo?
George Washington was the first president of the United States.
Who was the second?
Gatorade was the first sports drink.
What was the second?
Neil Armstrong was the first person to walk on the moon.
Who was the second?

Another immutable law is the Law of the Mind that states that it's better to be first in the mind than to be first in the marketplace. Obviously, if perception is more important than product, then the mind takes precedence over the marketplace. Influence and persuasion are less about what you are saying, than *how* what you are saying is perceived, received, and understood.

To buy the hearts and minds of the customer we must know what balls to pitch. While decisions are most often based on emotions, we need to avoid the pitfall of an either/or dichotomy where we divide all consumers into a left-brain or right-brain category as if the world is all engineers or artists.

Personal values will determine if a product is an emotional right-brain buy or an analytical left-brain decision. For example, cars are said to be an emotional buy but for many it is just a means of getting from point A to point B. Getting a laptop that allows me to write my books is a dry decision, but a left-brain "techie" becomes passionate and excited about all the bells and whistles on the computer he buys.

Energetic Communications: Surface Versus Subliminal Messages

Communication is the core ingredient to all relationships both personal and business. Certainly in sales and leadership, we need to be in sync with our team and our clients or customers. We communicate on a variety of levels such as verbal and nonverbal which are both based on our physical senses and is referred to by Bob Scheinfeld in *The 11th Element* as "surface communications." Bob refers to what we experience with our non-physical senses, intuition, sixth sense, or gut instinct as "energetic communication." When the two channels conflict and provide two different messages, we feel confused and withdrawn due to mistrust or a disconnect. That's when you lose your connection and potential business. However, the energetic, subliminal messages will override the message on the surface communication channels. Do a check on all your written and verbal communications and make sure that both channels match and are in sync with the other to keep your message strong, powerful, and direct. Powerful communication occurs when the two channels match and reinforce the message of the other.

Synchronized selling is being "in tune" with your clients or team by speaking their language. By taking a whole-brain approach to selling, you appeal to more people and diverse thinking styles. Research indicates that people experience more pleasure when all functions of the brain—the senses, emotions, thought processes, and intuition—are engaged and stimulated. The more the mind is involved and must search for a conclusion, the more positive and enjoyable the experience. The mind's active participation has its own reward. Besides, we are always more committed to conclusions that are our own. Leave something to the buyer's imagination and allow them to "fill in the blanks." It gives them permission to sell themselves and prevents a serious case of buyer's remorse.

Management professor Charles Margerison identified four conversation patterns observed when people try to influence each other:

Four Conversation Patterns

1. Persuasion Effect—One side successfully persuades the other persons to adopt or agree to their position.

2. Negotiation Effect—A negotiated compromise results when neither party can totally persuade the other. The gap is closed.

3. Fixation Effect—Both sides take up fixed positions and refuse to compromise. Differences are reinforced and the gap widens.

4. Polarization Effect—Both sides unfairly attack the other's position to establish their superiority. The polarity increases as they continue to talk.

In addition to conversation patterns, persuaders must also know their own thinking style and, more importantly, know how the person they are persuading processes information. For example, if you are persuading an innovative visionary person who easily buys into the excitement of new opportunities and future trends, you must speak a different language than when convincing an analytical thinker who prefers facts, figures, and statistics.

Likewise a humanitarian "people" person may be hopeful that creating harmony and a warm relationship will motivate the other to honor a handshake, while organizers will insist on everything being in writing and will insist on dotting the "I" and crossing the "T." On the other hand, if a number cruncher presents impressive data to convince an emotional/feeling person, there will no impact because they won't bother to even read the research. It's simply not what motivates them to take action. However, once they trust you and a bond is formed, they will follow you anywhere. There are four types of persuaders based on one's brain dominance which directs one's communication style:

Four Persuasion Styles
1. Innovative Visionaries—Future oriented (upper right brain)
2. Humanitarians—Feelings oriented (lower right brain)
3. Analytical Thinkers—Facts oriented (upper left brain)
4. Organizers—Form oriented (lower left brain)

In addition to understanding differences due to brain-dominance and thinking styles, it is also important to recognize differences in values, attitudes, and motivators affecting buying behaviors due to various generational groups.

Zap the Gap: Baby Boomers, Gen X, Gen Y
It is essential that you get into your customer's head, determine their motives, tend to their values and desires, and then trigger their emotions which will compel them to action. Are you speaking your consumer's

language? In *Emotional Branding,* Marc Gobé discusses the three growing generational influences in most economies today. The baby boomers, the Gen X, and the Gen Y groups each have distinct attitudes and motivators. The following includes some of the values, mindset, and experiences of each group.

Baby Boomers

Baby boomers, born between 1946 and 1964, number 81 million strong and spend over $900 million annually. SPAM (email) reflects how retailers are trying to capture this market because it is so big. If the baby boomers played the stock market well, they have lots of money that they want to spend restoring their youth, their health, and their enjoyment of their final decades. From hippies to yuppies, from flower children to preppies, these people are watching the replays of *Happy Days* or fighting for a cause that became their identity during the sexual revolution and the protests or riots of the sixties.

With aspirations running high, they respond to achievement, status, and authority and may still wear their monogrammed cufflinks for sentimental reasons (however, many of them do it out of habit because they worked for IBM when it was mandatory). Reflecting the "Us" philosophy, they are realistic and their attitude is, "I earned it—I deserve it." Thus, fortune building and prosperity are motivators. They tend to be couple-oriented, for in college, they were "pinned" and engaged, and soon after graduation, they were married or the relatives became worried (especially if you were female).

Gen X

Born from 1965-1976, with only 46 million members, this group spends $125 million annually and is a bit self-centered with "I" being the center of their universe. Many have experienced their parents' divorce and thus have learned to become quite independent and defy traditional structures. They are a "take-charge" entrepreneurial group that is highly-educated, money-driven, and loves luxuries and life's simple (but expensive) pleasures. Spas, manicures, and massages were almost non-existent back in my day. These Gen Xers' concerns about physical health began the routine of "going to the gym," and jogging became a morning or evening ritual. If they don't go to the gym, they at least put it on their New Year's resolution list and buy the membership. Rather than sex, sexiness is valued, so Victoria's Secret came out of the closet and into the bedroom on more than just Valentine's Day.

With the information revolution, this group was exposed to harsh realities such as cocaine, gang violence, and AIDS. Thus, they tend to be pessimistic and seek solace in their idols and celebrities. They replace the aspiration of their parents with inspiration, and religion with spirituality.

Gen Y

With the "All" philosophy, Gen Y people are great team players (for many had soccer moms). Born from 1977-1994, they are 75 million strong and spend no more than $100 million annually. Reared in the era of psychology, positive mental attitude, and self-help, they are fun, optimistic, and thrive on unity and community.

New ideas excite them and their curiosity makes them interesting and learned. They have a marketing savvy and are fascinated by mysticism and worlds beyond. After all, space travel was now a reality, while for me, *Captain Video* was a Saturday morning cartoon. Their parents are their heroes rather than some rock star. They have a global mindset and demonstrate social responsibility, including a respect for the environment. Rather than sex or even sexiness, they are more focused on sexuality and rather than being male-female, they are people-oriented.

As minds continue to change, so must you unless you want skinny kids. More than just knowing trends you must learn to anticipate them or as the champion hockey player Wayne Gretsky said, "I go where the puck is." In sales, marketing and branding is crucial to understanding your market and to speaking their language in order to have influence and impact.

I have found *American Demographics* to be an excellent magazine on market trends, as well as the online newsletters, *Trend Setters* and *Growth Strategies Newsletter*. In *Brain Tattoos*, Karen Post gives great advice on how to use branding effectively:

> *Go where your market lives today and where your buyers will be tomorrow. Brand leaders who understand the entire spectrum of their buyers and not simply the narrow need they may fill with their brand will ultimately succeed. Branding is not about a simple transaction, but a relationship. Do you treat your market*

like a good friend you know well, or like a stranger on the street? Brand communications is a two–way dialogue. It's ongoing, and it's about speaking in your buyer's language and providing relevant information that improves their lives and connects to their deepest values.

Hugh Rank developed a model for out-thinking your opponent in the persuasion process by effectively directing your attention.

- *Intensify your strong points*
- *Intensify your opponent's weaknesses*
- *Downplay your own weaknesses*
- *Downplay your opponent's strengths*

Intensify Your Strong Points

1. Repetition of the strong point. Often referred to as the broken record, repetition creates a laser-like focus and has a hypnotic effect.

2. Association with an established credible person or product. Our unconscious mind blurs and thinks in terms of patterns and associations. This is why Nike pays Michael Jordan millions to wear their shoes. People believe when they wear the same shoes as Michael, they will be a bit like him and score from all over the floor. It takes more than wearing it on your T-shirt, but in a world of push-button love and instant success, it appears to be a reasonable shortcut.

3. Composition of the message massaged for maximum impact. Ronald Reagan mastered the art of composition like no one else. He choreographed his messages for television such that you tuned in whether you liked him or not. His background as an actor certainly helped.

Downplay Your Weaknesses

1. Omission of damaging information. Politicians use omission all the time, at least until they get caught. Omission includes the half-truths that the tobacco industry presented for decades until the whole truth was revealed.

2. Diversion by shifting the focus away from weaknesses to strengths. President Bill Clinton mastered diversion and shifted attention to his trip to Africa when the media was more interested in his relationship with Ms. Lewinsky.

3. Confusion by using jargon and faulty logic. Often referred to as "double talk," when people are confused they simply throw in the towel to relieve their discomfort and concede out of exasperation. (Beware. Other times they "walk" to alleviate the pain of confusion.)

Knowledge of the other person's mind state is essential. How your message is perceived is determined by their existing attitude. If their attitude is positive, there will be a high level of acceptance, while a negative attitude predisposes one to rejection of a new thought. Those who are neutral and non-committed can be skillfully persuaded. An example is the OJ Simpson verdict; 77 percent of African Americans were in agreement with the verdict. However, 65 percent of white Americans disagreed with the verdict, and if that same poll were taken today, that percentage will have increased substantially, even among the African-Americans whose attention was skillfully diverted to the case being a racial issue rather than a murder case.

When persuading a group or audience rather than one-on-one interactions, you must know your audience and their diverse makeup. Present your argument with diverse speaking styles to connect with each one at some point in the program.

Persuasion Pointers for Groups and Audiences

1. Know the level of acceptance and rejection or the hostility, neutrality, or receptiveness of the group.

2. Establish credibility with evidence and testimony. Don't promise all things to all people which will dilute your credibility.

3. Set realistic, achievable goals with gradual step-by-step changes.

4. Inspire a supportive group to compel them to action.

5. Convert a neutral group by selling benefits.

6. Educate the uninformed audience with a logical, easy-to-follow presentation.

7. Motivate and energize an uninterested audience with stories, compelling facts, and highly relevant information.

8. Neutralize a hostile audience by establishing credibility and solid evidence of information presented.

9. With a mixed audience, focus your pitch on the subgroup that has the most power.

10. Make it safe to change without losing "face" or damaging egos.

To influence group change, the science of Axiology offers an objective way to assess and understand how the "values" of a company's managers and employees impact team performance. As a leader, manager, or sales trainer, the insights derived from the values assessment will not only help you understand, manage, and motivate your team, but also guide you in proper placement and selection to reduce the unnecessary expense and financial losses of employee turnover.

The "systemic" perspective demands that employees' first loyalty is to their jobs and a paycheck should be sufficient reward; the "extrinsic" value is evidenced by the employees' focus on gaining a "return on investment" for their willingness to go the extra mile. An "intrinsic" value emerges when people decide they want to be treated with respect and to be valued for their unique worth as individuals.

There is no fixed formula for influencing, persuading, and managing others. In fact, the differing values of executives, managers, and employees can affect working relationships and thus your company's performance. As I had previously mentioned, the changing values are often a generational issue. A few decades ago, employees were glad to get a job and keep it. They valued security and believed that their hard work would provide well for their families and their future retirement. Their children, the "Baby Boomers," saw their parent's dedication not paying the desired dividends. Entering the workforce more highly educated, the Baby Boomers demanded much more for themselves in terms of opportunities, benefits, and promotions.

Then "Generation X" observed the mistakes of their parents who were so focused on success and getting ahead that they had little time for themselves or their families. As Generation X was about to enter the workforce, they saw their hard-working parents and neighbors suddenly laid off in the name of mergers, downsizing, or a "flattening" of the company pyramid.

Generation X thus became the "now" or "me" generation with a somewhat self-absorbed orientation to life. Self-indulgence and putting one's self first became more important than putting money in the cookie jar for retirement, and personal freedom replaced security.

To measure your own thinking process, go to www.raether.com to take the values assessment which has been the most insightful tool I have personally experienced. Success is a conscious choice. Rather than reacting to consequences, you can choose to be in control of the thoughts that influence change and produce the desired results you deserve.

Persuasion Tactics

- Stop selling and telling; start partnering and positioning. Position both your product and your credibility in the prospect's mind.

- With integrity, appeal to the three basic motivators: fear, greed, and exclusivity.

- Be first—not best, but first.

- Listen to first understand and then to be understood.

- Trust your intuition and develop your sixth sense to get in sync and in tune with yourself and your customers.

- Allow buyers to sell themselves. Engage their imaginations to fill in the blanks.

- Know your audience and be flexible and diverse to first connect and then lead them by skillfully directing their attention to the chosen conclusion

- Success is a conscious choice. Don't react to consequences, rather choose the results you deserve.

Chapter Four
The Principle of Expectation and Attraction

We love to expect, and when expectation is either disappointed or
gratified, we want to be again expecting.
Samuel Johnson

The Law of Attraction reveals how your subconscious mind works for you by focusing on the *essence* of what you want, rather than on the appearance of something, and thus magnetizes you to receive what you truly desire. We are all familiar with the quote by James Allen, "As a man thinketh in his heart, so is he." However it is the "how" one might think that reveals the secrets of true wealth, which is attainable through understanding the natural relations between mental action and material conditions. In other words, by your habitual thoughts you create corresponding external physical conditions that attract the nucleus that then attracts to itself its own correspondence.

God Will Provide the Food, But He Will Not Cook the Dinner

An experience Gandhi had when discovering his purpose and developing his vision well illustrates the Law of Attraction. When a man arrived from a distant country and volunteered to join Gandhi, he asked Gandhi if he was surprised at his unplanned appearance. Gandhi simply replied, "When a person discovers what is right and purposeful, and begins to pursue it, the necessary people and resources tend to appear, as if attracted to the cause." Gandhi is a supreme example of influence and resonance, for he never had any official position in government or business, had no wealth, and commanded no armies. However, he influenced, mobilized, inspired, and transformed millions of people.

The power of expectation is revealed in numerous studies with varying names. Most people are familiar with the Placebo, the Pygmalion, and the Halo Effects which all verify the power of expectation and suggestion. In the 1970s, psychologist Dr. Robert Rosenthal revealed how the expectation of one can alter the behavior of another. Students of the same IQ were randomly divided into two groups and teachers were told that one group was gifted and had high IQs, and that the other group was dull and had low IQs. After only eight months, the supposedly high IQ group performed at an A level while the supposedly low IQ group performed at a D level. The only variable in the study was that of the expectations of the teachers involved.

There are numerous studies in medicine where the Placebo Effect has, in some cases, been more effective than the medication given after negative side effects of the medication were taken into account. Studies have shown that people often get better just making an appointment with their doctor. They continue to improve and symptoms subside even while sitting in the waiting room. I guess if they wait long enough, they may not even need to see the doctor. Now, that's a clever way to cut healthcare costs. In another study, doctors performed a false surgery for breast implants, and although there was no actual surgery, the breasts were increased because of the patient's expectations. In the Korean War, there was a shortage of morphine to relieve the pain of suffering soldiers. Thus, doctors gave sugar pills and suggested that their pain would soon be relieved and approximately 25 percent of the soldiers reported a reduction in pain.

Your brain is not your mind, but your mind's instrument, just as your body is the instrument through which thoughts and feelings are expressed. Your mind is the envelope of the soul. A positive, confident, expectant mind renders you receptive to creative forces. It is because of the receptive nature of this divine creative faculty that thoughts are manifested and you become unstoppable. Faith is the unseen world and thought that gives substance to things unseen. You can actually think of only one thing at a time, thus, you cannot have positive thoughts as negative words are spoken. Select your words carefully for they predict your future success.

Elizabeth Browning states, "We carry within us the wonders we seek without us." However, all of life's forces can only manifest to the degree that you confidently believe that they can and will materialize. The intricate reciprocity of your mind and the Universal Mind is the key factor to how and when we blossom. This integral relationship was confirmed by Genevieve Behrend in her interviews with Judge Thomas Troward at the turn of the century, "God will provide the food, but He will not cook the dinner." Co-dependent relationships don't work in life nor in the symbolic world. Things are symbols, and it is important to remember that the thing symbolized is more important than the symbol itself. Remember also that the mind is not fickle. If you start and end your day with a well-directed meditation, but the rest of your day is filled with fear and anxiety, you are sabotaging your success. Judge Troward continues to explain to his pupil that "will" is a thought stabilizer and holds a thought to a given purpose until it is consummated or manifested. He insisted that you get into the spirit of your desire. "The spirit of a thing is that which is the source of its inherent movement."

Analyze Divine Spirit and You Darken the Light

There is no limit to the creative power of your subjective mind once you have impressed it with your intention. Your subjective mind receives its impressions from the objective mind and never from material things. Therefore, it is necessary to withdraw your thought from the material or physical thing you desire and to mentally dwell upon the spiritual symbol of it, which is the inherent source of its formation. Purer intentions are more readily received by your unconscious mind as it instantly passes them forward into the Universal Mind. Unless your faith is built upon the solid foundation of absolute conviction, you will never be able to make practical use of it. By holding the thought of what you are, you guide yourself into what you want to be. Troward also affirmed: "One should regard his individual subjective mind as the organ of the absolute, and his objective mind as the organ of the relative." What flows through things is atomic energy; through animals is instinct; and through man is thought. If you analyze the Divine Spirit, you will darken the light. Living Spirit is not found in a book—you must practice it.

We observe that atomic energy or Divine Spirit in people who radiate with a magnetic charm. There is a dynamic countenance about them, a nobility, a noticeable confidence, a poise that sets them apart from everyone else. They work, think, act, and speak from an internal reserve of composure and confidence which engages and captivates. They remain centered, spontaneous, and rise above the circumstance as if sustained by *something*. When they walk into a room, they *own* it! You can *feel* their presence. When under pressure, they are able to respond with even more grace and poise as they rise to challenging occasions. Certainly that Divine Spirit was demonstrated by both survivors and victims of 9/11. Todd Beamer's call to action with, "Let's roll!" will linger on even though United 93 and all its passengers had no choice but to rise to the challenge of an inescapable fate. According to negotiation expert and author Roger Dawson, "Charisma is that rare quality, that *je ne sais quoi*, that causes people to fall under your spell, to want to follow you, to be with you, even when they don't know much about you."

While some people seem to be naturally gifted with charisma, it is not as much a genetic endowment as a skill that can be learned and developed. When Princess Diana first entered the public arena, she was a shy, awkward, young woman, who seemed uncomfortable with all of the attention. Diana learned, however, to tap into her inner reserve and project an air of confidence, nobility, and poise. From "Shy Di," she blossomed into an international icon of beauty, grace, and compassion. She didn't start out as "a natural," but developed a charisma that charmed the entire world (except for Prince Charles).

Charisma will provide you with an unfair advantage in business negotiations, sales calls, or simply convincing your children to finish their homework. To follow are suggestions on unlocking your charisma:

Keys to Charisma

- Your appearance is your "visual resumé." Make a powerful statement not only in your hair, grooming, clothing, eye contact, posture and carriage, but also in your *internal* posture. As Dr. Wayne Dyer points out, "If you are not responsible for your thoughts, then who is?" Make a firm resolve to be responsible for your state of mind in every waking moment.
- Create a sense of enthusiastic purpose and urgency about your ideas and projects. Charismatic people have an unwavering sense of purpose and are fully engaged in their projects and incurably optimistic about their goals. They radiate energy and are able to engage others in their charismatic aura.
- Wear your passion on your sleeve. Charismatic people exude an infectious magnetism that attracts others. Empower others and create a connection and an emotional bond by speaking their language. Be proactive. Let others know exactly what they can do to further your cause and give them permission to move forward.

- Resonate. Share compassion by speaking from the heart. Treat everyone you meet with the utmost care and unconditional positive regard. Charismatic people see the self-worth of every individual, whether that person runs the company or maintains the grounds. Make everyone feel they are the most important person in the world. Stealing a snippet from my own book, *Winning*, Margaret Thatcher shared a meal with President Ronald Reagan and Sir Winston Churchill. As she recalled the feeling of being in the presence of greatness, she noted that while Churchill made everyone feel that he was the smartest person in the room, President Reagan made *you* feel like you were the smartest person in the room. That's resonating.

- Have a generous spirit. Giving praise and paying compliments are trademarks of charismatic people. Give sincere, unsolicited compliments. Charisma directed by love and good purpose is the driving force of civilization and personal success as well.

- Maintain composure no matter what. Charismatic people know that chips on the shoulder can splinter deals, so they maintain their composure no matter what. They are tenacious but not presumptuous or arrogant and they refrain from boasting. Sales people who maintain their honor, respect, and composure despite a customer's objections or outright refusal will reap the returns of the Law of Reciprocity. It will come back to you. Composure is a sign of confidence, self-control, and character—all traits that raise your other IQ—Influence Quotient.

- Send clear, concise, consistent messages. Charismatic people send one message when they communicate their intentions, without hidden agendas. They don't send mixed messages which cause confusion and withdrawal, for a confused mind always says, "No."

- Take lots of calculated risks. In *Winning!*, my interviews revealed that the one thing all champions had in common was their extensive experience with losses. To a champion, however, a loss or failure is simply feedback to correct and forward the action plan. Losses and setbacks are stepping stones to success, but only when perceived in that light. Sometimes the line between calculated risk and folly is transparently thin, but charismatic people know that healthy risks more often than not lead to greater success and fulfillment in life.

- Set life boundaries. Highly successful charismatic people practice what I call purposeful impatience. They value principle, cooperation, and integrity and are impatient with poor performance and lack of effort. Whatever field they are in, they draw a line for unacceptable behavior and hold that line with their clients, their team, and their families.

- Charismatic people hold conversational dialogues, not monologues. They listen thoughtfully, ask questions, give feedback, remain objective, interested, and are fully engaged and present. Humor is their conversational condiment that adds spice to every relationship and provides comic relief. Humor also helps to keep things in perspective.

- Keep communications simple. Reduce complex ideas into simple messages. Charismatic people have a remarkable ability to flip complex ideas into a simple message using symbols, metaphors, analogies, and stories to resonate well.

Just as influence is emotional intelligence at its best, charisma is influence at its best. Without charisma, influence is like a balloon without air—lots of potential but no action.

To make things happen you must be committed to going the "extra" mile, for the difference between extraordinary and ordinary is the "extra." With charisma and commitment your magnetic point of attraction will always be toward what you want. The question is, "What do you want?" In *The Attractor Factor*, Joe Vitale reveals how your inner state of being attracts and creates your outer results—and what to do about it so you can have, do, or be whatever your heart desires. He explains that the shortcut to creating the life you want is to be happy now. If you can be happy right now, in this moment, you will have achieved whatever you want because underneath everything you say you want is the desire for happiness and happiness is a conscious choice. What creates the outer, which is just an illusion, is your inner. Vitale sites Paul Ellsworth's 1924 classic book *The Mind Magnet,* in which he states, "Consciousness is cause." A.K. Mozumdar states it another way: "Mind operates under its own conception of itself.."

You must transcend your fears to manifest miracles. You may have to go to a new playing field to change your complaints into a personal action plan and thus transform your problems into possibilities.

Fear is a wish you don't want which Elinor Moody stated in *You Can Receive Whatsoever You Desire*: "Let us remember that fear is only wrongly directed faith. We are having faith in things we do NOT want, rather than in the things we desire." What are your beliefs? How will you change them? Again, what do you want? What would you be doing if you knew you couldn't fail? What service can you provide and how will you make a difference?

In *The Spontaneous Fulfillment of Desire*, Depak Chopra writes, "Intention is not simply a whim. It requires attention, and it also requires detachment. Once you've created the intention mindfully, you must be able to detach from the outcome, and let the universe handle the details of fulfillment." Thus you must be clear on what you want without needing it or being dependent upon the outcome for your joy and happiness. Struggling to achieve something causes a backlash and triggers opposite forces. Rather with confidence assume your victory from a place of peace and inner serenity as you flow to your fulfillment.

Vitale echoes the wisdom of so many others with a five-step formula to having it all:

Five-Step Formula to Success

1. Know what you don't want.
2. Select what you do want.
3. Clear all negative or limiting beliefs.
4. Feel what it would be like to have, do, or be what you want.
5. Let go as you act on your intuitive impulses, and allow the results to manifest.

As you take full responsibility for your experiences knowing that you attracted them, you will be personally empowered to change your thoughts and beliefs so that you stop sabotaging and start supporting your personal desires and dreams. Rather than disapprove or dismiss the truth, learn to embrace it.

"Man is a magnet, and every line and dot and detail of his experiences come by his own attraction." – Elizabeth Towne, *The Life Power and How to Use It*.

Persuasion Tactics

- If you revel in adversarial relationships, it is better for you to go into arbitration, wrestling, or criminal law, because the world of buying and selling is not for you. Buyers and sellers are not on different sides. Today's best sellers use their charisma to influence customers to flow with them in a win-win dynamic.

- The "twelfth sale" is a metaphor for thinking ahead. If you establish your initial buyer/seller relationship as a partnership in which you are thinking ahead to the twelfth sale and not just the current event in the customer's buying cycle, you will have the right mindset for multiplying your sales efforts. Think of the twelfth sale.

- Logic makes people think, but emotion compels them to act. Buyers may react to your reasoning in defense of the features and benefits of your product or service, but when they *feel* that you are an invaluable asset, they will invest in you and become a raving fan.

- Confidence and positive expectations trigger a "Yes" response. A potential client proudly announced an eight percent growth for the past three years. I asked, "Why wasn't it twenty percent," showing my confidence that his firm could do better. That expectation got me the contract to do their sales training.

Chapter Five
The Principle of Perceptual Contrast

There are two kinds of people, those who do the work and those who take the credit. Try to be in the first group. There is less competition there.
Gandhi

When the contrast between alternatives is great, it is easier to convince people to take one path rather than the other. The differences between two opposing ideas are more apparent when the ideas are presented at the same time and the contrasts are emphasized.

Years ago I heard of a young Girl Scout who broke all records by selling thousands of boxes of the yummy Girl Scout cookies. An obvious master of the art of sales, a curious group questioned the young girl on her success strategies. She simply answered that she would knock on doors and ask people if they were interested in buying tickets to the Fireman's Ball for $25.00. Apparently too many people felt like that was a steep donation since they did not dance and would never cash in on their purchase. The Girl Scout then offered her Girl Scout cookies for $2.00 a box and most bought several boxes being relieved by the lesser investment. Even the health-conscious were tempted by the tasty delights. This also confirms the theories that people feel obligated to buy something and are more apt to buy what you present last, especially if it is the least expensive.

I have also heard that the young Girl Scout was on the Johnny Carson show and reported that her secret was that she began by asking for a $30,000.00 donation to the Girl Scouts and then relieved their anxiety by asking if they would at least buy a box of Girl Scout cookies. Rumors get twisted over the years, but the power of contrast is clear. Her system was simple. She created a conflict in that she was adorable and people wanted to buy something from her, but would hope to achieve resolution for less than the high-priced tickets to the dance. She then offered a solution to the very problem she created. The contrast of the prices made it easy to order several boxes.

Reality Is Based on Comparisons

You may have heard of the college student who had sent her parents the letter reporting a series of disasters in her life including a skull fracture from her jump out the window when her dormitory caught on fire. She then confessed that she was pregnant, with the father-to-be being less than desirable. After giving her parents a near-death experience story, she then continued to announce that there was no fire, no skull fracture, and that she was not pregnant, but that she did get a "D" in American History and an "F" in Chemistry, asking that they put her grades in proper perspective. Although Chemistry may not be her thing, I am sure she passed Psychology with flying colors.

Let me share a personal experience with how I allowed myself to become a victim of the persuasive powers of contrast. A slick real estate agent showed me million dollar oceanfront houses, now in excess of five million dollars, in Wilmington, North Carolina. At record speed, the realtor then rushed me up the coast about thirty miles to North Topsail Island where, at that time, land on the ocean was worth 1/10th the market value of land in Wilmington. The high-speed chase up the coast made it feel even closer. The opportunity seemed so spectacular by contrast to the prices in Wilmington, I bought several! It created a financial disaster, but his skillful presentation of the principles of contrast made one feel like a fool if you did not sign on the dotted line. The contrast principle affects the way we see the difference between two things that are presented in sequence, with the second situation perceived even more differently than it actually is.

Certainly when we dive into a swimming pool, the water temperature is perceived differently in contrast to the temperature of the outside air. Our emotional and physical pain is often soothed and comforted by the more severe misfortunes of others. When you fear the diagnosis is cancer but then find out that you only have the common cold, you celebrate having a cold. (I am certainly not recommending that doctors use this technique with their patients.) Our experiences of reality are based on contrast and our perceptions of comparisons.

Start high. Fundraisers usually ask for donations half the size of your paycheck but then will settle for $5.00 or whatever you choose to give. This way you get to ease your conscience and still pay the bills. Timing is crucial for if there is an extensive lapse in time, the effect is lost. In sales it is suggested that you sell the more expensive item first, whether it is a car or a suit, and then the accessories and upgrades will be added on because, in contrast to the price of the major item, the extras or add-ons are an easy decision. "What's a few bucks more?"

A few practical suggestions to apply the Principle of Contrast would be to start high. Realtors do it all the time. Timing is also crucial here for if there is too much of a time delay between requests, the comparison is lost and so may be the deal. Certainly the current situation must be taken into account as what is appropriate depends on the individual's current frame of mind. In general, it is better to not throw in last minute surprises as people tend to be more cooperative when not feeling pressured or rushed. The hard and fast sell often will exasperate people so that a "no" answer resolves their problem and stress. When defenses are up, there is no compliance.

Presentation as a Persuasive Power

Contrast is also used to encourage sales by offering three "easy" payments or creating installment plans. Sometimes we are blind to the money we are spending as we become so directed to see only the opportunities provided or the money we are saving. Reframing one's perception of the value is also accomplished by breaking down the price to what you might pay per day rather than the lump sum or annual fee. It's all in how one looks at it, and as a master of persuasion, you guide others' perceptions by how you present the information.

Everyone loves a bonus. It alters our perception of the value. In a high school bake sale, 40 percent of the customers bought a cupcake and two cookies for 75 cents, but when the cupcake was sold for 75 cents and the two cookies were given as a bonus, then 70 percent of the customers made the purchase. While bundling is good, bonuses are better. The conclusion is that it is not the price paid, but the extras and add-ons that serve as triggers to action. What would you buy—a burger that is 75 percent lean or 25 percent fat? The power of suggestion rules, for the word "fat" caused consumers to perceive the same burgers as "fatty and greasy" or "lean and delicious" depending on what words were used to describe them. Presentation persuades.

Perception is the key factor. Perhaps you have noticed that the candy bar has shrunk and may have fewer almonds even though the price has increased. When altering price or quantity, it is less obvious to skim off an ounce or two rather than increase the price, especially if we maintain the size of the box. In fact, most boxes are half empty and are getting bigger. I recall my health-conscious son firmly reprimanding his daughter, Amanda, who was about to indulge in a piece of candy with the warning, "That's junk!" She quickly retorted, "But it's *good junk*," and continued to indulge. Perception is one's reality and it is all in the eyes of the beholder, driven by what they want and what they value. Forget reality.

Small doses allow people to swallow and come back for more. For example, as a speaker I am on a first name basis with most of the airlines that practice the "nibble" approach for crowd control. When there is a delay in departures, they will frequently avoid announcing a two-hour delay as it tends to ignite tempers. Instead, they announce a slight delay, followed by another delay, and then an announcement that the plane is on its way, and then that boarding will begin in another hour. How might you present information differently to your clients and your work team so they perceive opportunity and are motivated to take positive action whether that be buying a product or achieving higher levels of achievement and performance?

The fact is there are no absolutes, for everything is relative to something else which thus allows you to direct and manage perceptions. The "Just Noticeable Difference" (JND) theory suggests that we change things so slightly that the difference is so minimal it goes undetected and we still feel we are getting a deal. You may have noticed most of the two-quart ice cream containers have been downsized to 48 ounces.

Another form of contrast is the Comparison Effect which focuses on how the customer may compare two options simultaneously and come to the conclusion that the second option is more desirable. Anorexia nervosa has become much more prevalent since models have been wearing a size 4 rather than a 10 which had been the desired size for so many years. Research at both Arizona State and Montana State Universities have shown that spouses perceive their partners as less attractive after viewing pictures of models.

In *Influencing with Integrity*, Genie Laborde discusses how the mind can't process everything at once and thus develops shortcuts to help make decisions. By providing your clients with a benchmark based on their past knowledge and experience, you are giving them boundaries, patterns, and polar opposites so they can better compare and make decisions.

Subconsciously people have high expectations and selectively prefer the good over the bad, especially if they are right-brain dominant. However, the disappointing reality to follow their high anticipations may create a contrast that destroys all hopes for any sale.

None of us really operates in the "real world," for the entire process of perception, thinking, and communication depends on combinations of chemicals in the brain. These brain chemicals code and transmit our perceptions and thoughts into coded experiences on a map in our brain which then establishes our behaviors. Although the map determines our behaviors, we determine the map (which in fact is not reality other than as we choose to create it).

Influence and persuasion is about releasing all limitations in perceptions and the thinking processes that reduce both our own possibilities and our client's choices as well. Your effectiveness in influencing others is about opening doors to the unconscious which is where perceptions are rooted. Knowing that the unconscious has information not available to the conscious mind is empowering, for just knowing that you "know" more than you think you know can make a big difference in how effectively you communicate. *It is knowing you know what you don't know.* Hopefully you will now feel more confident in trusting your intuitive impulses and actions. Your choice of perceptions and words both contribute to the structure of your world. How you skillfully use those words structures how others perceive opportunities and possibilities in their world.

Persuasion Tactics

- Make contrasts dramatic and timely. Presenting contrasts at the same time produces greater impact and perceptual differences.

- Start high. You can always come down so everything less will be perceived as a "win" to your customer.

- Nibble—nibble—nibble. Present price and information in small doses. Break down the price using methods such as installment plans. Skillfully craft your presentation to guide perceptions and thus persuasion.

- Give bonuses. While bundling is good, bonuses are better. Set a higher price for the lead item and present the other items as bonuses.

- Be positive. Avoid negative words and present everything in terms of "what is" rather than what something "is not."

Chapter Six
The Principle of Scarcity and Urgency

Easy things nobody wants, but what is forbidden is tempting.
Ovid

Most things are more appealing when they're in short supply. It's the economic principle of supply and demand. People are willing to pay a higher price when items they desire are rare, limited, or not readily available. When objects of their desires are scarce and/or their window of opportunity is short, people are more apt to take prompt action.

We all want what we cannot have and want to hoard when things appear to be scarce. It is instinctual to become a bit greedy and grab all we can before it's gone. We become like squirrels gathering acorns for their long winter's nap. The survival instinct prompts us to take action even though we may survive very well without the purchase. The forbidden fruit is always tempting. The prohibition of alcohol developed many entrepreneurial "spirits" who met the increasing demand for alcohol because attempts were made to make it extinct.

Value Is the Essence of Opportunity
If there are limited editions of artwork, the price automatically increases, not because of the quality of the art but because the supply is limited. Bargains suggest opportunities and right-brain people thrive on opportunity which is not the same as greed. Value is the essence of opportunity that appeals to our competitive sense to feel like a winner while greed evolves from a selfish desire for more than what one needs or deserves. This is not only true of a want for material things, but also time, information, expert advice, and price. Ask Martha Stewart about the price one is willing to pay regarding expert advice on trading secrets on stock investments. But then, Adam and Eve paid an even higher

price for not resisting the forbidden fruit. The reason children always want the toy they cannot have is they've had lots of good teachers. Although wanting what we can't have is learned, it is also instinctual and the nature of the beast.

Back in my youth, young girls were encouraged to "play hard to get" to be perceived as a more desirable date. Not only do most opportunities now come with an expiration date, buying on E-bay or online now has a clock ticking away, allowing just minutes to cash in on the prize. Opportunities always seem more valuable when they are less available. It is amazing how many times the same furniture company has a going-out-of-business sale! While we like "free," it also diminishes perceived value. Frequently it is when vendors double their prices for the same products or services that business increases.

Another frequent strategy is when toy companies will announce limited supplies just before Christmas (think of the announcement regarding the limited availability of PlayStation a few years ago). Another incident of intentional scarcity as a marketing ploy was back in the mid-nineties. Tickle Me Elmo played the same trick of promoting the doll and then deliberately limited production to drive up the prices. People were selling dolls they had purchased for just $30.00 for over $500.00. Some parents need to learn to say, "No." Trust me, your child will survive and will not be psychologically maimed by the word "No" or life without Elmo. Besides, kites rise highest against the wind and as parents you will be delightfully blown away by the psychological resilience your children develop from healthy negligence.

Masters of this manipulation are some real estate developers who host weekend fantasy property parties along the sunny coast. I recently attended such an event in North Carolina where every half hour another bus full of eager buyers from the North arrived. Seeing everyone in a buying frenzy, grabbing lots selling for a minimum of $200,000.00 as if they were buying gumballs certainly gives the impression that time is of the essence. When your ten minutes of viewing the property is up because another group is coming in to buy if you don't, your instincts kick in and the urge to seize the opportunity is beyond resistance. To confirm how scarce the lots are the developer is quick to put SOLD signs up immediately and probably puts up a few extra ones for good measure (or based on wishful thinking). The principle of social proof is also in process, for when you see all these seemingly intelligent, sophisticated investors buying up three and four lots at a time, the conclusion drawn is they must know something you don't and thus you follow the herd.

Sensing the similarity of this situation to a previous time when I had been swept away by promises of scarcity, I did my due diligence and fortunately was able to get my deposits returned to me. When you feel caught up in a wave of emotions based on fear of losing out on an opportunity or scarcity, let it be a red flag that waves you into a state of calm as you reconnect with your rational mind to regain a balanced perspective.

Fear of Loss Motivates Action

To encourage action, less is best and the fear of loss is even more motivating. Achieving greater health, energy, and vitality always sounds inviting, but the real moment of truth and change comes when one may lose it all. People don't quit smoking to breathe better but to prevent losing a lung or even their life. If you're willing to walk away from the sale, it will probably be yours. If you have ever visited Mexico, you probably discovered how quickly the price can come down when you aren't interested or are willing to walk away. Losing a "potential" sale feels the same as losing the actual deal. Imagination can be perceived as reality. More energy is put into defending what you have and not losing it than acquiring something that is not yet yours. Having romance is enchanting, but losing the love of your life can be devastating.

Certainly people with the "collectors" mentality well illustrate the excitement created by owning something rare, whether it is a precious antique or baseball card. Imperfections and mistakes with time have increased value simply because they are rare or one-of-a-kind. In the same light, we seem to put more value on the call we just missed—until we realize it was just a telemarketer.

One of the most innate desires and cross-cultural values that we universally uphold is freedom. People die for freedom, not only their own but for the liberation and freedom of others as well. As things become less accessible, we are threatened with the loss of freedom to choose, to have, and to hold. Certainly Shakespeare's Romeo and Juliet defied all boundaries by taking their own lives to find freedom together. It is not only during the "terrible twos" and teenage years that we resist and react to restrictions. This innate need to declare our independence was discovered by the tobacco industry decades ago by creating the macho Marlboro man who died from the toxic product he promoted. Virginia Slims appealed to the rising women's liberation movement by creating the image and the jingle, "You've come a long way, Baby." Unfortunately, they were most successful in their lengthy campaign that increased the percent of cigarette smokers in only one U.S. demographic group—teenage women.

Get Them to Do It—Forbid It

Censorship is another example of how people react not to the issue but to the act of restricting freedom. Reverse psychology is foolproof. An example is when University of North Carolina students learned that a speech opposing coed dorms on campus would be banned. The students became more opposed to coed dorms without even hearing the speech. To oppose the censorship of the speech that opposed coed dorms, many were now in support of an action they theoretically were against. If you have a teenager, you may have discovered that the best way to get them to do something is to forbid them to do it.

Add the element of competition and the desire for any commodity increases. The introduction of the blue light special by Kmart caused store stampedes that made some aisles danger zones. All those useless, unused bargains make for great rummage sales and tax write-offs.

Add the element of exclusivity and people really feel they can't survive without the distinguishing factor that nourishes the ego. More expensive and exclusive country clubs tend to have the longest wait lists even in a "down" economy. I remember buying gold necklaces thirty years ago for twice what I could purchase them for today, but there was a rumor that the price of gold was going to make it functionally extinct and thus I opted for bread and water so I could stock up on all that overpriced gold. Other luxury items seem to become more essential during tough times. Joy perfume advertises its high price as a selling factor and it works. Not everyone can afford Joy—therefore everyone wants it.

Swindlers do polished presentations on the scarcity scheme. Years ago I received a call from a no-name Wall Street investment group whose sales representative spoke like a train was chasing him to convey a sense of urgency. His whispering voice clearly communicated that you were among a select few being offered this inside secret on a stock about to soar. Then, in his second call, he gave a strong sales pitch followed by the haunting news that the opportunity was no longer available, causing you to feel like a rabbit in heat. With well-timed precision, the final call offered resolution to your agony with an unexplainable last minute opportunity to still cash in on the prize. Fortunately, my son who works for Morgan Stanley, a very reputable firm, was visiting at the time of the unpaid drama and reminded me that not all people have my best interest in mind.

There are three magical words that trigger our instinctual brain to grab quickly:

Act now!

One day only!

Limited supplies!

("Limited supplies" is the most powerful and effective.)

According to philosopher Jim Rohn, "Without a sense of urgency, desire loses its value." To sustain the perceived value fueled by desire, master persuaders are sensitive to what motivates the public and the subtle changes in patterns to better anticipate future trends in the marketplace. Influencing factors are never fixed and always subject to change. If the world is changing, are you?

Although my primary focus has been on how our thoughts and style of communications influence the actions of others, the social and economic environments also influence behavior patterns. In *TRUEWEALTH*, Steve Sjuggerud reports that the stock market has about a seventeen-year cycle that illustrates how the thinking of the times affects whether we experience a bull or bear market. There is a dynamic cause and effect cycle between the collective consciousness of a culture and its financial and societal circumstances. .

Frequently we respond with a knee-jerk reaction to what we have learned from those around us, especially our parents. For example, people who lived through the Great Depression (from 1930-1947) and lost everything would be hesitant to invest in any stocks, but would rather hide their money in a cookie jar, or buy Treasury bonds. Folks who invested in stocks during the 1950s and made a 500% return believe that stocks only go up, only to be rudely awakened by the dark years from 1965 to 1981 with harsh memories of Black Monday.

To be one step ahead of the game, whether it is the stock market and our wealth building strategies, our personal relationships, or our career choices, we must learn from the past and gain wisdom from history, yet liberate ourselves from a fixed-pattern response. Instead, we must boldly move forward influenced by our own conscious choice.

The same is true in marriage or other committed relationships where we bounce from one extreme to the other in our choices for a partner. If a quiet, stable, responsible husband becomes boring and lacks excitement, he may be exchanged for a more charming, fun, flashy, free spirit who forgets where home is and can't keep a job. In becoming more aware of both internal and external factors directing behaviors you can then out-think and more effectively persuade others.

Persuasion Tactics

- Be exclusive. Resist being "too" available.

- Have the courage to walk and say, "No."

- Be believable. Don't sound too good to be true.

- Freedom: Give it but also take it away.

Chapter Seven
The Principle of Commitment
and Consistency

The moment one definitely commits oneself, then Providence moves too.
Whatever you can do or dream, you can begin it.
Boldness has genius, power, and magic in it. Begin it now.
Goethe

Once a stand is taken and a commitment is made, all unconscious forces mobilize our actions and behaviors to be consistent and in alignment with that commitment. Commitment versus just involvement is well illustrated by the analogy of ham and eggs. Obviously, the chicken is just involved, but the pig is committed. The fact is, once we commit to a certain course of action, we are then committed to continue on that course and remain consistent to our established decision. The longer we are invested in our decision or commitment and announce it publicly, the more we tend to defend our stand. That may be why President Bush, whether right or wrong, will continue to stand strong and defend his commitment to fight the war with Iraq and the war on terrorism.

We Decide by Emotion and Justify It with Logic
The Halo Effect reflects how we resist any disruption to our image or original belief system. Celebrities such as OJ Simpson may receive favorable judgments due to people's stubborn loyalty to their idols and heroes. President Bill Clinton's polls actually had shown an increase in support when the truth about his affair and perjury became known. No one dared to openly discuss President John Kennedy's mistress, Marilyn Monroe, until after his and Jackie's deaths. We all had to let go of Camelot before we could face reality's heartbreaking disappointments. Princess Diana is another icon of how we remain steadfast to our ideals

that may have been instilled by our favorite fairy tale. Perhaps Snow White ought to get a cut from the profits of computer dating services that benefit greatly from people's loyalty to the myth that a kiss from the magic prince or princess shall suddenly bestow happiness upon us.

We decide by emotion and justify it with logic. Our defense mechanisms play an active role in helping us to maintain a sense of sanity in our sometime insane decisions so that we can feel good about our choices. For example, if we pick the wrong stocks or buy real estate at the wrong time, we often remain loyal to our demise rather than cut our losses. This instinctual drive for constancy and consistency with our past decisions quietly, but powerfully, directs our behavior and the behavior of others and thus is a powerful tool for influence and persuasion. To be a master of the art of influence, it is imperative to understand the functions of the instinctual brain, referred to as the Old Brain by Patrick Renvoisé and Christopher Morin in their book, *Selling to the Old Brain.*

It is amazing how many of my classmates are returning to their roots as they begin to retire. I grew up in a small fishing village in rural Wisconsin and although we had a bumper crop of kids who have planted seeds of success all over the country, most are coming back home to their real roots. Not surprisingly, 70 percent of people remain in the same religion they were raised in as children despite living in a world of continual change. Behavior is not that difficult to predict if we simply observe patterns that are continually repeated. Unfortunately, it is also why so many smokers, alcoholics, gamblers, and criminals return to their paths of the past. Prevention is always easier than the cure. Establishing strong, positive behaviors at an early age is crucial.

In *The Science of Influence,* Kevin Hogan cites a study that confirms how our commitments strengthen by writing them down and making a public announcement. As we transform thoughts, ideas, and goals from the abstract to the concrete, we are literally transforming our thoughts into actions and our dreams into reality. It has worked for every winner and champion I interviewed in *Winning!,* and it will work for you *if* you work with it.

A research study had subjects make decisions among various choices. Group A was asked to "remember their decision." Group B was asked to "write their decisions on a magic slate and then pull the sheet up, 'erasing' their decision." Group C was asked to "write down their decision on paper with ink and hand it in to the researchers." As you may assume, Group C stuck with their decisions more than three-quarters of the time, while Group B kept their decisions half the time, and Group A tended to change their minds.

Cognitive Dissonance: Minds Hate Confusion

Because minds hate cognitive dissonance (when there are two opposing thoughts at the same time), we often act impulsively and make decisions to resolve the discomfort. Too often our behavior is on autopilot and, because we are imitators, we are quick to act out what the movies, MTV, and the commercials suggest (a very disturbing thought). Powerful suggestions are often implanted in questions and in "how" these questions are asked.

Exceptional lawyers such as OJ Simpson's lawyer, Johnnie Cochrane, and Michael Jackson's lawyer, Thomas Mesereau, are perfect examples of how the way questions are asked can sway the focus and thinking of the jury to get them all to say, "Yes." Whether on the side of justice or not, an exceptional lawyer is a master hypnotist who, with subtle suggestions, controls the minds of the jurors with a secular spell. There are several jurors from the OJ Simpson case and also jurors from the Michael Jackson case who are regretting their decision declaring the defendants as innocent. When the smoke has cleared and one is no longer under the "influence" of masters of sway, thinking becomes clearer and more objective, but then it is simply too late. When the verdict is in—time's up!

CEOs are paid outrageous salaries for their ability to think and make decisions, hopefully good ones. Not to decide is to decide. Just as we cannot *not* communicate, so too, we cannot *not* decide. This is a lesson to be skillfully applied as a negotiation strategy as well. The moment of decision is the moment of change, and not one second before.

New Year's resolutions are too often not a sincere decision or commitment, but simply a sweetened annual wish list ritual which is why so many claim the same resolutions year after year after year.

People quit their jobs and start their businesses, write their books, lose weight, or quit smoking when they "decide" to take that first step. Decisions direct actions and thus understanding the mental process of decision-making is essential to the persuasion process. Although these internal forces for homeostasis hold us captive, we are also influenced by external pressures such as the hopes and expectations of others. Children master the art of influence early on with, "You promised!" (It certainly keeps the toy companies profitable.)

Commitments Are Wings to Change

Decisions rooted in conviction and commitments are our wings to change. Commitment is obviously a powerful and sometimes threatening force which may be why the "Now" generation prefers to just live together rather than be bound by the commitments of marriage. On the other hand, people often remain in unhealthy, toxic relationships simply because they have made a decision and commitment and are driven to be consistent with that choice even though it literally may be killing them. Denial and rationalization often times rivet us to our commitments and frequently deny us access to our own truth.

Sometimes we buy impulsively when there is emotional appeal for fear that when reality sets in and logic is revealed, it could deny us from what we simply "want" to do. If we want it, we will find a way to get it, even if we have to play games with our minds to do so. For example, if you are searching for your soul mate, many who profess to fit the profile will be accepted by your mind as the ideal partner simply because you have projected onto that person all that your heart desires. When we are seeking solutions or salvation, there will always be lots of charlatans ready to take your money and help you feel good fast if you can trust their unwritten guarantee.

Applications of the Principle of Commitment and Consistency

Commitment

Get a commitment up front and get it in writing. Harley Davidson gets their loyal customers to tattoo the Harley Davidson logo on their chests— now that's low-cost advertisement and commitment. One could not even consider riding a Suzuki with a Harley logo on his chest. Whether writing down your personal goals or establishing loyal customers as a salesperson, your expectations must be clear and well-communicated, followed by written validation of that commitment. The written contract is not just for legal and business purposes, but it mentally and emotionally focuses energies. Make it public. Public commitments are lasting commitments. Certainly Alcoholics Anonymous (AA) uses the power of public confession, as do many religions. Weight management, smoking cessation, and other programs to overcome addictions also use the power of the public confessional.

Compliance

Compliance begins with the foot-in-the-door technique. Convert your prospects to customers with small commitments or sales that can then build to bigger sales. We mold and shape behaviors by setting smaller commitments and creating a new identity and definition of self. If you get people to "stand for something," it is more difficult for them to then sit down. While our actions and behaviors are a result of who we are, our actions also define us, and in turn predict future decisions and behaviors. Our smaller agreements and commitments create a blueprint that our psyche follows with blind obedience and thus builds a compliance mentality. Once we make a smaller commitment, we then justify and support it with larger commitments. Commitments are self-sustaining and self-generating. We believe in and follow our actions more than our words. While compliance is often a concession to external pressures or threats creating short-term change due to fear, commitment is an internal choice—a change from the inside out and thus is more permanent.

Low-Ball Technique

The low-ball is where an advantage is offered that induces a favorable decision to purchase. Then, before the bargain is sealed, the original purchase advantage is mysteriously removed. Despite the original grounds for the decision crumbling, the deal does not collapse since it is only one piece of the pie, and the customer justifies his decision by recalling all the other features and benefits. This tactic actually makes people feel good about their poor choices. Once the sale is made, people then sell themselves in defense of their decision. However, if people perceive the low-ball technique as a bait and switch, the deal may be lost. Deception does not nurture trust and is not influence but fraud. Be careful how you use this one.

As a consumer, when you feel the external pressure to be consistent and true to your word, but your intuition or sensory feedback system has a nagging feeling in your gut, you need to take heed and tune inward. When you are being gently nudged down the path of compliance and you are screaming internally to get out, it is probably a "no-win" situation where forced compromise will not bring resolution. So get out!

To fully understand influence, Dr. Leon Festinger's *Theory of Cognitive Dissonance* must also be understood. The theory reveals what happens when a person's behavior is dissonant from her beliefs and attitudes. Dr. Festinger developed four paradigms to better understand patterns in dissonance reduction. Leaders and managers must implement the principles of these findings by creating challenge, involvement, and full participation on their respective teams.

Four Paradigms of Cognitive Dissonance

The Free-Choice Paradigm
The post-decision dissonance states that negative aspects of the chosen alternative and positive aspects of the rejected alternative become dissonant with the decision. Vice-versa, the positive aspects of the chosen alternative and the negative aspects of the rejected alternative are now consistent with the decision. The more difficult the decision, the higher the level of dissonance. Reduction of dissonance will be attempted by removing the corresponding negative or positive aspects. Altering the aspects of these decision alternatives to reduce dissonance will lead to viewing the "chosen" alternative as more desirable and the rejected alternative as less desirable.

The application of this principle is to get all objections from your client or team members on the table so that they can be dealt with or resolved. As you anticipate such dissonance you can dissipate it.

The Self-Consistency and Self-Affirmation Paradigm
The Self-Consistency Theory assumes that situations that induce dissonance do so because they create inconsistency between self-concept and behavior. Most people believe in their own positive self-image and therefore are likely to experience dissonance when behaving in an immoral fashion. For example, if you see yourself as an honest person, lying would create dissonance and discomfort. This is why learned and earned self-esteem is critical to a moral society.

The Effort-Justification Paradigm

Dissonance arises when a person is placed in a situation that involves unwanted or unpleasant activity that yields a desirable outcome. It is stated that from the belief that the activity is unpleasant, one would not engage in the activity. The cognition that the activity is unpleasant is dissonant with engaging in the activity. However, research reports by Aronson and Mills indicated that the women who suffered more severe, embarrassing activities for initiation into a social group evaluated the group more favorably than those women who were in "mild" initiation activities. This may explain the addictive cycle of women (and men) who continually return and remain in abusive relationships. They simply have more time, history, energy, and their own selves invested. It's perhaps why blood runs thicker than water.

The Induced-Compliance Paradigm

Dissonance arises when a person says or does something that goes against a prior belief or attitude. The belief is that the person would not engage in the behavior, yet promises of reward or threat of punishment provide cognitions that are consistent with the behavior. The dissonance can then be reduced by changing the belief to better reflect what was originally said. For example, a health-conscious person who smokes or is overweight may justify their habit rather than change their behavior. A frequent rationalization is, "We all have to die sometime."

In personal and business relationships, it is imperative that we get an investment or personal involvement of the other person's time, energy, or money in the desired outcome. It is always more difficult for both the buyer and the seller to walk away from a sale when the negotiations have been extensive and both have been intensely involved in the process. However, there is a point of fatigue and exhaustion where we walk from potential opportunity simply because we are stressed out by the process. People quit their well-paying jobs, leave marriages, and take early retirements when the fatigue factor becomes greater than the justification.

Persuasion Tactics

- Get a commitment up-front. Get it in writing. Carve it in stone. Make it public. People are fiercely loyal to their commitments and their tattoos.

- Pitch to emotions—the old, instinctual brain. It's where decisions are made.

- Being creatures of habit, as a leader and salesperson you are shaping behaviors—a good one is getting to "Yes."

- Ask questions that will direct the focus and thinking of your customers for the desired outcome.

- Never promise more than you can deliver. Never!

- Convert prospects into customers by throwing a low-ball and getting smaller commitments that lead to compliance on bigger commitments.

- Get objections on the table. Anticipate dissonance so you can prevent it.

- Get an investment—time, energy, money, and thought.

Chapter Eight
The Principle of Social Consensus and Conformity

The greatest difficulty is that men do not think enough of themselves; do not consider what it is that they are sacrificing when they follow a herd.
Ralph Waldo Emerson

When making decisions, we follow the ethics and guidelines of our society, community, and culture for support and direction. We pay the price of compliance to satisfy the need for inclusion and affiliation. People are mirror reflections of each other's beings. Perhaps keeping up with the Jones's is less about status and more about inclusion and social conformity.

Everybody's Doing It
Social consensus is about *monkey see—monkey do* and the adage, *Everybody's doing it.* The Principle of Social Consensus affects how we make decisions. We view a behavior as correct in a given situation to the degree that we see others performing it. We all seem to have the herd mentality that is not exclusive to cows and a pack of wolves. After delivering an inspiring keynote, if someone in the front row rises to his feet, the rest will follow. If someone in the back of the room stands up to give the much deserved standing ovation, no one sees her stand up and thus no one follows. Often feeling somewhat embarrassed, she will quickly take her seat. Taking the dance floor demonstrates the same need for permission from the masses. Once a few couples take to the dance floor, those waiting to wiggle without being conspicuous quickly find themselves dancing the disco.

When was the last time you chose a restaurant when not a soul was dining there? Certainly there would be no wait and you would be showered with service, yet instead you choose to go down the block where the wait is thirty minutes. The answer is obvious. If everyone else is doing it, it must be good. While often true, how many times have you been mislead by that assumption? You often stand in the longest line, spend hard-earned money on fad clothing, and put holes all over our body if the gang says it's the cool thing to do. How many times have you been standing in the wrong line for no good reason other than that's where the line was and everyone was standing in it?

Much of social etiquette is learned by social consensus. If you are confused as to what fork to use at a formal dinner party or whether to eat your pizza without one, you simply check out how everyone else is maneuvering their food from plate to mouth and follow the unwritten protocol. When streets are cluttered with litter it is much easier to drop your trash there as well than when sidewalks are sparkling clean. When tipping the driver of the airport shuttle, you sneak a peak at what the pilots are tipping, for they should know what's expected.

Voluntary Brainwashing

Certainly the principle holds true with the masses and explains the violence of gangs, terrorists, cults, and people such as Jim Jones. (I dropped the "Reverend" as he doesn't deserve the title.) Jones was the self-anointed spiritual leader who demanded the mass suicide of 910 people in Jonestown, Guyana in 1978. He prepared a vat of strawberry-flavored poison and, with the exception of a few who had resisted or escaped, most very willingly followed suit after the first woman gave the poison to her child and then to herself. Social consensus, conditioning, and compliance can even override the survival instinct. I call it cultural override which is also witnessed in the suicide bombers of the terrorist groups. As Walt Disney suggested, "People look to you and me to see what they are supposed to be. And, if we don't disappoint them, maybe, just maybe, they won't disappoint us."

Voluntary brainwashing is when we willingly choose to follow the crowd and thus create a new norm. We are concerned about the behavior of our children's friends knowing that it will influence who are children become. If their friends smoke, drink, or take drugs, your child is at high risk. Because others choose to have dinner, we often do the same even when we are not hungry which contributes to the obesity epidemic in the United States. How many times do you ask your dining partner what they are having before giving your order. And if you are a woman, you may even take a survey of other women present to solicit a bathroom buddy (a strange version of "follow the leader").

Traditional advertising and infomercials all increase their credibility by presenting endless testimonials that all seem to say the same thing, but if everybody is saying it, it must be true. Cavett Robert, our beloved founder of NSA (the National Speakers Association), suggested the following. "Since 95 percent of the people are imitators and only 5 percent are initiators, people are persuaded more by the actions of others than by any proof we can offer." The more people doing it—the stronger the impact and influence. When a fundraiser comes to the door asking for a pledge, it is always harder to refuse a donation when you look at the list and see that every one of your neighbors had given quite generously. The momentum creates a tipping point.

Uncertainty Breeds Conformity

Conformity is the disease to please. Depending on when you were born, the mantra for many is, "What will people think?" Conformity is much like consistency in that it is the desire to be consistent with your peer group's acceptance and is as important as oxygen during the teen years. Fashion trends, however, make a great deal of money on people who get stuck at that stage and never evolve into a self-defined, independent human being. Advertisers prey on people who lack identity and crave image. Even nonconformists and rebels by society's definition are people conforming to their group's nonconformist standard. Just ask any gang member.

While conformists make up about 85 percent of the population, only about 10 percent are contrarian conformists who rebel against societal norms. The third group is the contrarians who are neither conformists nor anti-conformists, but rather true independent thinkers and entrepreneurs.

An interesting study by Milgram, Bickman, and Berkowitz clearly illustrates Cavett's suggestion. When they had just one person stand on a busy street and look up in the sky or at a tall building, no one really glanced up but just walked on by. However, when four friends also looked up, within a minute about 80 percent of all passersby lifted their gaze and joined the crowd. When there is uncertainty, we become even more apt to accept the actions of others as truth. This phenomenon is called pluralistic ignorance. We frequently hear of attacks in broad daylight when there are hundreds of passersby who never stopped to help the victim, simply because no one else did. We see with the eyes of others and from their response or lack thereof, we allow those social clues to determine our perception of the situation. In larger cities, indifference and apathy become survival mechanisms. It appears that when there are more potential helpers available, the personal responsibility of each person is diminished.

Early morning talk shows can be more annoying than the slow moving traffic when Dick and Jane giggle more than they speak and you're still trying to figure out when you missed the punchline. To boost their ratings, *Saturday Night Live* and all television productions employ laugh tracks or canned laughter as they have been proven to be positively contagious. We tend to assume that if everyone is laughing, it must be funny and thus join in. (I personally change the channel.) It also provides a safety net for poor jokes that bomb, although most should blow up. I love good, creative humor and quick wit, but I am finding it a rare commodity in entertainment today and I *don't* follow the crowd.

Remember, your current judgments and decisions are based on current beliefs and societal norms as well as past experiences. Don't limit future possibilities by stale thinking and stagnant information. Think up. Imagine tomorrow.

Persuasion Tactics

- Use testimonials from celebrites and people perceived as experts or successful.

- Create a norm. Suggest behavior patterns by initiating them yourself. Professional pianists put the first dollar in the tipping jar.

- Identify the leaders and key players. Get the queen cow to moo and the herd will follow.

- Know your herd, but don't be one of them. Rise above. Think up!

Chapter Nine
The Principle of Benevolence and Reciprocity

You can get everything in life you want if you will just help enough other people get what they want.
Zig Ziglar

According to renowned social influence researcher Robert Cialdini, by virtue of "the law of reciprocity...people feel obligated to make future repayments of favors, gifts, invitations, and the like." This sense of obligation occurs in all societies, in all age groups, and at every socio-economic level. Anthropologists view this "web of indebtedness" as the foundation for the bond of interdependence between people that makes societies work. Paleoanthropologist Richard Leakey has long maintained that the essence of what makes us human is our benevolence, and that our ancestors' survival depended on "an honored network of obligation." Strategic benevolence is so powerful a persuasion tool that it's almost like creating a vacuum causing what you want from life to flow to you. A Japanese saying sums up the law of reciprocity quite succinctly, "Nothing is more costly than something given free of charge."

Free Donations Are Never Free
Obligation is a simple persuasion technique that goes back to the Fuller Brush man who went door-to-door handing out free samples of their infamous brush. Currently we are offered free samples of tasty treats in the grocery store that lure us into buying the whole cake. The waitress who adds a mint to the tray as she presents the bill receives a bigger tip and if the manicurist adds an extra coat of polish, we tend to add to her tip as well. When people go a bit above and beyond the call of

duty it is perceived as a gift from the heart that triggers a generous spirit in us. Realtors get new listings by offering a free market analysis. Free donations are never free. How many times have you attended a free lecture or presentation, but then the hat was passed asking for a donation after the program or a strong pitch was made to "purchase" their forthcoming seminar?

The Hare Krishna movement discovered the power of obligation when donations were low because of being perceived as counter-cultural. When the solicitors first gave a flower that they refused to take back, many who did not believe in the cause gave money simply because their sense of obligation compelled them to reach inside their purses and give something in return.

However, all tactics of benevolence must be perceived as sincere and as unselfish acts rather than as a bribe or pressure tactic or compliance will actually decrease. That is why in a negotiation process if you are going to give a gift it must be given *before* the negotiations begin and not during the process or your gift becomes an obvious bribe. If you ever use obligation to manipulate others, you will lose all credibility and all that you might propose. Only *losers* manipulate to win.

One Good Turn Deserves Another

In *Maximum Influence*, Ken Mortensen refers to a story that succinctly reflects the power of reciprocity. During World War I, some soldiers were given a special assignment to make sorties into enemy territory in order to capture and question enemy soldiers. A particularly skilled German soldier was instructed to fulfill one such mission. As he had on numerous other occasions, he negotiated the area between fronts and caught an enemy soldier off guard, eating his lunch alone in a trench. Unaware of what was happening, the startled soldier was easily captured. Not knowing what else to do, the soldier tore off a piece of bread and gave it to his captor. The German was so surprised by the friendly gesture that he couldn't follow through with his assignment. Turning away from the soldier, he headed back into neutral territory and on to face the wrath of his superiors. The adage "one good turn deserves another" is obviously a part of social conditioning in every culture. In fact, the mental or psychological debt is often so great that we often dramatically exceed the original favor given to us.

Another example cited by Mortensen was a study done at Cornell University by researcher Dennis Regan who had two individuals try to sell raffle tickets to unsuspecting workers. One individual made a conscientious effort to befriend the workers before attempting to sell any tickets. The other individual made a point of being rude and obnoxious around the workers. While on a break, the individual who had previously been rude to his prospects bought them drinks before trying to get them to buy tickets. The results of the study showed that the rude individual actually sold twice as many raffle tickets, even though the other person had been so much nicer and more likable. (It obviously takes more than a warm smile.) Of course, the emotional burden we can place on others by our "giving" spirit is often abused and misused which is why many women refuse that free drink at the bar when approached by an eager male with an ulterior motive.

When you help people get what they want or need, you create a sense of obligation that makes them indebted to you out of an innate and universal sense of fair play. Even when you change your mind to see things from another's perspective, they in turn will be more cooperative and begin to see things your way and change their minds because you did first. Perhaps if our political figures in government would learn these simple give-take lessons in life, we truly would have peace on earth.

This kind of giving creates tremendous "yes" responses to your requests, because people feel compelled to return a favor. Even if we don't particularly want or ask for a gift, favor, invitation, or unsolicited compliment, we feel a sense of obligation to return the favor. Being indebted to someone, even someone we don't know, creates such psychological discomfort that we sometimes go to extraordinary lengths to remove the burdensome obligation. Sometimes we even cringe upon receiving a gift from a neighbor, knowing that we will now feel obliged to respond in kind.

Getting Them to Nod—"Yes"

When someone smiles at us or pays us a compliment, we generally feel a need to return the smile or praise. Their smile is an obligation trigger that induces our fixed action response—a smile back. Sales people are taught to use the "Sullivan Nod" which is smiling and slowly nodding at the customer when suggesting an option to purchase. More than 60 percent of the time, the customer will nod back and concur with the salesperson's suggestion. Simple physical movements and observations can have a profound effect on how we feel and think. In fact, in a study by Gary Wells and Richard Petty, it was determined that "television advertisements would be most effective if the visual display created repetitive vertical movement of the television viewers' heads (e.g., a bouncing ball)." Thus, persuasion has less to do with obvious eloquence and verbal messages and more to do with the subtle, the hidden, and the unspoken. It is much harder to insulate ourselves against the insidious.

In politics, the exchange of favors makes local, state, and national politics beds of opportunities for strategic benevolence. It's common knowledge that campaign contributions "buy" favorable responses from leaders caught in a web of indebtedness. The same holds true for other obligation triggers such as free trips, tickets to special events, and expensive gifts. Supermarkets try to work this angle when they give us free tastes of food items, hoping our sense of obligation will lead to purchases.

Some people have learned to take and take without a sense of obligation to reciprocate, but the majority of us want to remain in the mutual benevolence circle. Since the insensitive ones are always in the minority, strategic benevolence remains a highly effective and legitimate sales strategy.

Another very effective benevolence trigger involves reciprocal concessions on the part of both buyer and seller. When a sweet 10-year old Girl Scout comes to your door, explaining that she only needs a few more sales to win the contest, how does anyone say no? In my case, knowing that the cookies would find their way to my hips, I declined, with pangs of guilt. "Well," she said, "if you don't want cookies, why don't you just make a small donation to the Girl Scouts? You'd be helping me and girls all over America." Now I felt obliged to make a concession, because she had made a concession. The tendency to reciprocate a concession with a concession is a primordial response.

Sometimes strategic benevolence produces a double-win. In an interview I included in my book *Winning!*, a disgruntled man in a Milwaukee pub (and Milwaukee certainly has a few of them) announced that he did not have a single problem that a thousand dollars would not solve. Emold, a stranger to the man standing at the other end of the bar, then pulled out a thousand dollars and gave it to the man stating, "There aren't a million dollars that could solve my problems." Feeling guilty for taking the money and obligated to return it, months later the man finally found Emold to return the gift of a thousand dollars. Emold was so impressed with the man's character and good intentions that he hired him as his warehouse manager for over fifteen years. Perhaps the principles of benevolence and reciprocity could be a new strategy for selecting and hiring only the best employees.

When You Lead...Will They Follow?

Until recently, strategic benevolence was not used very well in leadership circles. Leaders could learn a lot from benevolent, savvy salespeople. Although new emphasis has been placed on coaching, counseling, and self-managed teams to convert top managers into servant-leaders, many companies are still saddled with managers who are leery of employee participation and empowerment.

Those leaders who add strategic benevolence to their best practices have realized that taking care of their people pays back huge dividends. You cannot legislate discipline, loyalty, or exemplary job performance to employees, but you can win their hearts and their loyalty will follow.

Common Traits of Highly Effective Managers

- Refrain from personal attacks or saying unkind things.
- Don't give negative feedback when you are tired.
- Go out of the way to clear performance roadblocks for your employees.
- Keep the promises you make.
- Constantly reward people and send them honest expressions of appreciation and praise.
- Accept people for who they are.

Strategic benevolence works with families and in friendships too. Helping loved ones get what they want creates a sense of mutual indebtedness, loyalty, and harmonious relationships. One of the most vicious social cycles in life is the merry-go-rounds families put themselves on because of the petty jealousies and animosities that have been inbred and perpetuated. It happens in intimate relationships as well. When strategic benevolence is a strong family value, harmony is inevitable. Strategic benevolence can work especially well in nurturing family environments because the emotional mind share is already well established. It's in the family DNA.

A few years ago, Senator Kohl said something that haunted me. At the time he was on the U.S. Senate Hearing Committee on the Crisis in Math and Science Education. Kohl lamented, "There are young people out there cutting raw cocaine with chemicals from the local hardware store. They are manufacturing new highs and new products by soaking marijuana in ever-changing agents, and each of these new drugs is more addictive, more deadly and less costly than the last. How is it that we have failed to tap that ingenuity, that sense of experimentation? How is it that these kids who can measure grams and kilos and can figure out complex monetary transactions cannot pass a simple math or chemistry test?" The resourcefulness of these kids illustrates that motivation is fueled by what we value and what we believe serves us well. The kids in question did not experience the strategic benevolence and reciprocity of a loving, nurturing relationship at home and thus they are only able to project what they know and have experienced—exploitation and abuse for one's own self interest. As parents, applying our influence at home is even more important than in the marketplace as it is the core of all character building.

Both in your personal and professional endeavors, reciprocity is contingent upon the Laws of Intention. It is only when we give with a free heart and no strings attached, without an ulterior motive, that it comes back to us. If giving is motivated by what we can get in return, it is *not* giving. Don't play games with spiritual laws. Keep your game playing at the casinos where you have a much better chance of beating the odds.

Power vs. Force by David Hawkins presents profound research on the anatomy of consciousness and the Laws of Intention.

Since power is what makes us strong and force makes us weak, love, compassion, and forgiveness are empowering while revenge, judgmentalism, and condemnation are reduce our strength and thus we must give up weak attractors for strong attractors. Successful solutions are based on the powerful principle that resolution occurs not by attacking the negative, but by fostering the positive...power unifies. Force polarizes...power is associate with that which supports life, and force is associated with that which exploits life for the gain of an individual or an organization. Winston Churchill never needed to use force with the British people: Gorbachev brought about total revolution in the largest political monolith in the world without firing a shot; and Gandhi defeated the British Empire without raising a hand in anger...This reminds us of the observation of advanced spiritual teachers that the devotee has only to discover... that which he already knows. Force is the universal substitute for truth...The accompanying state of mind is quite distinct from the thrill of success; it is a joy of peace and oneness with all that lives...If top performers are imbued with the belief that their excellence is not a personal accomplishment but a gift belonging to all of mankind as a demonstration of man's potential, they will go strong and remain so through any event. True success originates within, independent of external circumstances. Every word, deed, and intention creates a permanent record. There are no secrets; nothing is hidden, nor can it be. Our spirits stand naked in time for all to see. Every act, thought and choice adds to a permanent mosaic; our decisions ripple through the universe of consciousness to affect the lives of all. Everyone's life, finally, is accountable to the universe...Compassion is the doorway to grace and to the final realization of who we are and why we are here, and of the ultimate source of all existence.

Persuasion Tactics

- Resolve ways to reciprocate by meeting a favor with a favor. Do favors as often as possible, thereby laying the groundwork for reciprocal benevolence to flow back to you.

- Practice making reciprocal concessions so it becomes natural and easy for you. This tactic, skillfully done, will bring you immense influence.

- Launch a strategic benevolence campaign at the office, at home, and at your civic club or trade organization.

- Since you cannot legislate discipline, win the hearts and minds of others through benevolence and the loyalty will follow in both your personal and business life.

- Help twelve people get something they want. Do that sincerely and tactfully and you'll have twelve people obliged to do the same for you. The principle is well illustrated in the movie *Pay It Forward*.

- Benevolence is not a bribe. Manipulation is thievery. Bribes and manipulation sabotage long-term success.

Chapter Ten
The Principle of Full Engagement

Without involvement, there is no commitment. Mark it down, asterisk it,
circle it, underline it. No involvement, no commitment.
Stephen Covey

Without involvement there is no commitment and without participation there is no involvement. Participation increases acceptance of the conclusion you are suggesting. It reduces the psychological distance between the start and the finish line. If you buy tickets for the football game, you are obviously less likely to watch it on TV.

Ways to Engage, Involve, and Receive Suggestions

Ask Questions
Negotiation experts Reil Rackham and John Carlisle observed that the more highly skilled negotiators asked more than twice as many questions as average negotiators. More than just giving us feedback, questions shape our destiny. When we ask questions, we create mental participation and thus engage the person. When questions are asked, they trigger the brain into an automatic retrieval mode to search out the answer or solution. By asking others to repeat the question, it becomes even more integrated and ownership of the issue is now transferred. Questions are also a softer way of confronting and making a point and thus reduce resistance and defensiveness to the issues addressed.

Certainly, leading questions guide your client to the conclusions you suggest and thus it is imperative to ask questions that evoke "Yes." How you word the question will vary your results. Leading questions not only affect the other's interpretation of the message but also what we remember and retain. To ease people into participating, start with the easier, broader questions first and then ask the more challenging, specific questions. Questions may reflect the power of suggestion, for when people were asked "how tall" rather than "how short" a basketball player might be, guesses were ten inches more. Asking for help or advice also engages people. In fact, rather than advising or just giving a hand, they plunge into the situation and claim total ownership.

Activate the Senses: Visualization

The more senses you activate, the more the brain is totally involved, thus increasing neural connections. What the mind sees the body believes, or as W. Clement Stone said, "What the mind of men (women) can conceive, the heart can believe, you will and shall achieve." Visualization and mental imagery provide a blueprint in our brain that triggers the unconscious mind and the RAS (reticular activating system) to focus and process 24/7 so that our dreams do manifest into reality. Hearing the praise after your achievement will propel you to even greater success. Feeling the joy of your personal victories creates new neuropathways that create a positive addiction to winning. Smelling and tasting are more difficult to integrate but equally important. The sixth sense, intuition, is a deeper level of knowing that incites us to move forward with confidence.

Physical Movement

Not only does saying "Yes" create a pattern of compliance and acceptance, but when people physically nod "Yes," they also are programming themselves to be more easily persuaded. People who have moved their heads from side to side in a "No" motion were resistant to suggestion and people with no movement at all were neutral. In fact, researchers at the University of Missouri found that TV advertisements were more persuasive when the images had repetitive vertical movements such as a bouncing ball.

Connect

When a salesperson engages a shopper into verbal conversation and is able to get the shopper to try something on, the chance of making the sale doubles. Perhaps the evasive "just looking" response may be the defense system and armor to being lured into the sale.

Atmosphere

Creating the right "feel" can make an environment seductive. Certainly a casino creates a different atmosphere than a hospital, but they both speak to us and make clear statements that determine whether we wish to linger or leave. Antique stores purposely maintain an atmosphere of disorder to make you feel like your digging through stuff for a rare treasure. It's creating the grandmother's attic experience. Depending on the effect you may be seeking, it may be better to create a relaxed or rushed atmosphere. For example, feeling "rushed" during a massage would certainly warrant getting a refund.

Music

Having done music therapy, I am happy to tell you that when music (not noise) is played, shoppers stay 18 percent longer and make 17 percent more purchases. Music is most effective when customers aren't really aware of it. There are some not so subtle rock bands that need to learn that lesson.

Aroma

Being the most primitive of our senses, smell is actually the most powerful in drawing us in or pushing us away. Cinnamon is one of the most pungent. Many studies have been done near a Cinnabon store and results have consistently reported that people spend more money and would be twice as likely to help people in need of change for a dollar. Realtors suggest their home sellers bake bread or chocolate chip cookies because the smell of such comfort foods often triggers wonderful memories. If scents did not have some "pull," why would people spend a couple hundred dollars for a small bottle of Joy perfume?

Competition

While some people withdraw from competition, other people are stimulated by the surge of adrenalin. People become motivated and united when set up against another group. Energy and excitement increases.

Attention

Startling statements, facts, quotes, movement, tips, examples, and questions will grab attention. The element of mystery and suspense will sustain it. Leave people hanging to pique their interest, as they will stay tuned to hear "the rest of the story." Newscasters use this technique all the time. Besides, people are more able to remember uncompleted thoughts because they have to participate and work for the answer.

If you lose people's attention, you lose all opportunity to persuade them. Adult attention spans are only about eighteen minutes, but even less for teens as the span seems to be decreasing with our brains being rewired for MTV, video games, and the remote control mentality. Boredom and confusion will trip the "off switch" immediately and getting attention back once you've lost it can be a challenge. Spare the details and don't oversell. Even a list of benefits (not features) becomes tedious. Stop selling and telling and start listening.

Become Familiar

Whether it is email, letters, posters, songs, or ideas, the more we see it, hear it, or relate to it, the more accepting we become. That's why we see the same advertisement day after day after day. Repetition increases awareness, understanding, affiliation, and retention. Persistence feeds repetition which is necessary for persuasion.

Try It On

Once we test drive or try it on, we become identified with a product and process and begin to feel identified with it and thus desire ownership. Experiential learning is always the most impactful because it invites people to try on desired behaviors. Role-playing provides an opportunity for people to persuade themselves which is always the ideal. When people sell themselves, there is no resistance and there is never a return or buyer's remorse. Trying on the future makes it easier to take the first step. It removes the risk factor. Teaching others is always the best way to learn. Thus as we sell others, so too we are sold.

Tell Stories

Stories stimulate the senses and the emotional right brain which creates greater impact and memory retention. Children aren't the only ones who love a good story. Because He spoke in parables, Jesus Christ is often referred to as the greatest orator of all time. People can relate to stories and thus project their own joys and sorrows into the drama that can bring resolution. Stories create a bond and an intimacy with your client or audience. They are a subtle form of persuasion where you can simplify the complex and persuade a group without detection. By using metaphors and examples in your stories, you can create visual images that invite people to participate in a shared world.

Persuasion Tactics

- Ask questions. If you don't ask—you don't get. To reduce resistance, present your statements as questions. Ask your customer to repeat your question.

- Get their attention and adrenalin. Be outrageous. It worked for Tiny Tim and Liberace—it can work for you too.

- Create an atmosphere that engages all the senses, especially one that is conducive to mental imagery and visualization allowing them to project possibility thinking.

- Get them to talk and interact with you as it initiates a bond and builds rapport. Get them to say "Yes," not only verbally, but with a positive nod as well.

- Become a storyteller who masters the metaphor. All great leaders and orators moved the masses with metaphors.

Chapter Eleven
The Principle of Authority and Association

Unthinking respect for authority is the greatest enemy of truth.
Albert Einstein

Association is the mind's shortcut to understanding as it allows us to make decisions based not on logic but on the linking of previous experiences to a current stimulus. Blind obedience to authority is another reflection of how our instinctual intelligence dominates our responses to requests even when obviously wrong. Perhaps that is why common sense appears to be so uncommon and critical thinking is rapidly becoming a lost art.

Symbols of Authority Convey Power

Although obedience to authority may appear absent in rebellious teenagers and gang members, the fact is they have an even greater sense of obedience to their perceived authority—the gang leader. The obedience of socially conscious Germans to Hitler's demands of destroying millions of innocent people is still difficult to comprehend. A national survey was taken after the trial of Lieutenant William Calley ordered soldiers to kill all inhabitants including infants and children in My Lai, Vietnam. The results of that survey indicated that over half the people (51 percent) said that if ordered to do so, they too would kill all inhabitants of a Vietnamese village. Such compliance is universal for obedience studies done in a variety of cultures all reported similar results.

Symbols of authority may carry the same power as the authority figure. Con artists have learned this trick well as they introduce themselves with impressive titles, wearing a pinstripe suit and red tie, and driving a pearlized pewter Cadillac (perhaps stolen). In fact, you can now purchase a "legitimate" doctoral degree without ever opening a book—just send in your money! I knew talk was cheap, but now even a college degree is as well.

Size, especially height in men, has also become a genetic status symbol. It was found in male engineering students that not GPA or IQ determined their starting salary but rather their height. The taller men started out with higher salaries. Since 1900, the United States presidency has been won by the taller of the major party candidates in nearly 90 percent of the elections. Likewise, tall men get more responses from the computer dating ads, although the response for women goes up as their height and weight goes down. A more recent study indicated that a woman's chances for marriage decreased with an increase in IQ, after a certain mean point I am sure.

Titles such as doctor, pope, or officer also symbolize authority. Being from the healthcare industry, I can relate to the frightening research to follow. We all have heard the familiar "doctor's orders." In research experiments, nurses were found following orders with gross over-prescriptions of unauthorized drugs. Even when an unfamiliar voice on the phone claimed authority with the title of "doctor," and ordered a nurse to administer 20 milligrams of a drug to a specific patient where the pill bottle clearly stated "maximum daily dose–10 milligrams," 95 percent of the nurses were about to administer the obvious overdose without any questions asked. It may be blind obedience that accounts for hospital errors as the eighth cause of death in the U.S., and a 12 percent daily medication error rate. I fly a great deal and am sure glad the pilots don't claim a 12 percent error rate or I would not be here to write books.

Clothing such as the uniform also commands compliance. The policeman's blue suit, the nun's habit, and the hospital whites (often green), as well as the business suit all command a degree of respect. Unfortunately, the scammers all exploit the attire advantage. Results from research in Texas indicated that when a man violated the law by crossing the street against the traffic light with a well-tailored business suit, three and a half times more people followed behind the well-suited jaywalker than when he wore just a work shirt and trousers.

Products are the Package and Product Combined

American's favorite status symbol is probably their car, at least for men. In a San Francisco Bay area study, motorists consistently waited much longer before honking their horns at a new, luxury car stopped at a green light than when behind an old, economy car. In fact, 50 percent of the motorists waited respectfully behind it, never touching their horns until it moved on. The lesson here is that we must all question the authenticity of posed authority by determining if they are truly an expert and if they are honest and operate with integrity.

The power of association creates its own authority. Michael Jordan and other sports heroes often make more money on their endorsements than they do displaying their true talent. When you buy Nike, you are really buying a piece of Michael or at least paying for Michael's house. Calvin Klein paid him $40,000,000 to do a few commercials on underwear, which is quite remote from dribbling and shooting a ball. However, people will pay more for any product if it makes them a bit more like their hero (or at least they think it does).

Marketing genius Louis Cheskin believed that people don't make a distinction, at least on a conscious level, between the package and the product and thus the product is the package and the product combined. When margarine was introduced back in the late 1940s, it was not the spread of choice probably because it was white and butter is yellow. However, when Cheskin colored it yellow and wrapped it in gold tin foil and put a crown on it calling it a classy name like Imperial, it passed the taste test and has been on your grocer's shelf ever since. As Paul Harvey would say, "And now you know the rest of the story."

Persuasion Tactics

- Project a powerful image. Peter Jennings did not graduate from high school, but as the anchor for *The Nightly News* with ABC, he certainly compensated by creating an image of credibility and integrity.

- Position yourself as the authority and associate your product with established brands and buying experiences. Don't flaunt degrees, symbols, and titles, but certainly use them. (Buying Victoria's Secret or other name-brand undies is not a symbol of success or power—except for limited circumstances.)

- Don't try to change minds, but rather adapt to them. Package your product with what people perceive and already know to be quality.

- Practice FutureThink™. Act "as if." Dress, act, and be the person to whom you aspire and wish to become.

Chapter Twelve
The Principle of Intuitive Selling
and Instant Influence

We leap to correct answers before there are sufficient data, we intuit, we grasp, we jump to conclusions despite the lack of convincing evidence. That we are right more often than wrong is the miracle of human intellect.
Donald Norman

The Information Age has never been referred to as The Knowledge Age. Information must be accessed, absorbed, understood, and integrated before it becomes knowledge. With the advent of telecommunications, the Internet, TV, cable, and computer technology, we are becoming somewhat paralyzed by information overload. In fact, we are becoming information adverse illustrated by our fight to defend ourselves from SPAM. We are putting more energy into keeping information out than into seeking it out.

Minds Can't Cope with Complexities and Confusion
The paradox here is that the same sophisticated mental mechanism that has created a fast-paced, complicated environment has forced us to revert back to the simplicity of our primitive nature to make decisions. While it is our high-level decision-making process and problem-solving skills that have given us a dominance on earth, the fast pace and information overload has caused us to develop shortcuts to prevent all circuits from shutting down. It is a system of physical, mental, and emotional survival. The mind simply can't cope with the complexities it has created. In a sense, we have mentally down-shifted from the cerebral, creative part of the brain to the levels of the emotional, intuitive, and instinctual brain for quick answers and a less fatiguing response to life's challenges.

Basic survival instincts such as the fight-flight response evolve from the instinctual, reptilian brain that puts us on autopilot with robotic behavior patterns.

Although it may give a quick fix, it often does not provide a solid solution. For example, the increase in spontaneous violence and shootings among our youth is due to a short circuit to the instinctual brain which is fast acting and impulsive; lacking foresight and reasoning. Due to high-pressure demands, we respond less holistically and make decisions on segmented, isolated bits of information, just like the lesser species because of their limited mental capacity. Prejudice is an example of how we may take a bit of information such as the color of one's skin and arrive at erroneous conclusions and judgments. Since our minds hate confusion, we make up our own conclusions to feel the comfort and closure of understanding an event. While it may lack truth, we feel better with the validation and support our lies and denial provide.

According to Robert Cialdini, "The ever-accelerating pace and informational crush of modern life makes...automatic influence and... persuasiveness increasingly important skills *now and in the future.*" Intuitive Intelligence: The Other IQ® is a term I trademarked when I introduced it in my first book, *Why Cats Don't Bark*. Developing your intuitive sixth sense has become increasingly important for effectiveness in sales, leadership, and life. Influential leaders rely strongly on their intuition or gut guidance in their decision-making, problem solving, and innovative thinking.

Intuition is derived from the Latin *intueri*, which means "to look upon... to see within." Webster defines it as "quick and ready insight... the act or process of coming to direct knowledge without reasoning or inferring." These standard definitions are good starting points, but they do not capture fully the power and potential of gut guidance. In a survey, 87 of 93 Nobel Prize winners claimed that intuition was primary to their success. G.W. Casper refers to intuition as psychic telegrams from the subconscious. Holbrook Jackson defines intuition as reason in a hurry, and Dr. Bernie Siegal describes it as that "something" in the body that hears messages and knows how to respond to them. It is our responsibility, however, to listen and respond. Our intuitive intelligence is not a Ouija board experience, but rather unconventional wisdom, a deeper level of "direct knowing," a reliable cognitive tool and sensory fact-finding system.

Buckminster Fuller called intuition "cosmic fishing." Bill Gates calls it "internal logic without walls." However you may define it, you have to put it to use, for it is vital to success, as shown repeatedly by the many accomplished people I interviewed in my previous book, *Winning! How Winners Think—What Champions Do.* Your intuition is right 100% of the time, it is just your interpretation that may get wires crossed and thus provide the wrong information. However you may define it, you have to use it for it is vital to success.

Gut Guidance and Intuitive Selling

How many times have you wished you had trusted your gut instincts? Maybe it was a personal decision such as choosing your life partner or perhaps it was a hunch about whether you should have made a right rather than a left turn in an unfamiliar neighborhood. It may have been the time you bought a lottery ticket, or perhaps you knew you were marrying the wrong person as you walked down the aisle. All of us have had those sudden inclinations or intuitive flashes I call gut guidance.

Unfortunately, such unconventional wisdom or direct knowing is often frowned upon by conventional knowledge. In the name of normalcy, society has taught us to be suspicious of intuition's truth and credibility. Many of us have learned to distrust our gut feelings. Sales training programs, therefore, follow conventional left-brain formulas and strategies that only emphasize "getting to yes," rather than also encouraging creativity and breakthrough thinking, which I call MindShift™.

Leadership in most organizations often makes the same mistake, treating employees as cogs in mechanized work environments, rewarding conformity and obedience to strict performance protocols. The havoc this plays with true productivity is seen in many companies as they struggle to meet the demands of an increasingly competitive marketplace. One script does not fit all. The template-type presentation restricts innovation, resonance, and influence in a prescribed sales pitch.

This goes back to the home and school environments where emotional and intuitive intelligence are misunderstood, undervalued, and discouraged. We have lost our natural ability to connect with untapped resources and undeveloped potential for we only use about one-sixth of our brain. (What a waste!) Until we explore and engage more of our brain power, which speaks to us through our intuitive flashes a lot more than we recognize, we will go on limping along on just one cylinder rather than six.

Gut guidance is essential to our success in effective persuasion because it provides mind-processing shortcuts that are essential for success in the age of blur and instant everything. With limited time for data gathering and processing, and increased stress in most people's lives, decision-makers, consciously or subconsciously, rely on shortcuts. We are being forced to be less analytical and more intuitive and instinctual in all decision-making. Unlike traditional linear intelligence, our intuitive intelligence is a sensory feedback system that is pivotal to mastering persuasion and appealing to current instinctual buying styles.

Sensory Selling: Quick and Ready Insights

It may help you to know that executive suites, sales offices, and well-appointed boardrooms have more in common with artists' studios and inventors' labs than you may think. In the *Harvard Business Review*, Henry Mintzberg of the McGill University Faculty of Management, reported the results of an extensive study of corporate executives from the fields of banking, healthcare, manufacturing, telecommunications, real estate, and hundreds of others. Mintzberg found that top management, operating under sometimes chaotic and often unpredictable conditions, usually relies on "hunches to cope with problems too complex for rational analysis." He concludes organizational effectiveness "does not lie in the narrow-minded concept called rationality, but in the blend of clear-headed logic *and* powerful intuition."

In one of his rare interviews, Ted Turner was asked about marketing analysis. He said, "There's never a good reason for a study if your idea is conceptually sound. I *never* did a market study on CNN's conception. I do my own instinctive marketing analysis." Fred Smith, CEO of Federal Express, believes that companies should rely more on innovation and intuition to survive.

I believe that purpose, passion, and persistence, powered by intuition and instinct is a persuasion miracle waiting to happen in this new era of sensory selling. One case in point is Shailesh J. Mehta's business philosophy. As Chairman and CEO of Providian Financial, a San Francisco-based financial services company, Mehta ignores traditional advertising, sales, and brand management. Instead, his people practice what he calls radical sales and marketing. He has been called a data Midas. He finds the right prospects through quantitative analysis, gets to know their buying preferences, then retains their interest, loyalty, and "wallet share" through his innovative practices and "sense for what the customer wants." Mehta insists there is no magic formula, but freely admits he has built his company's success on quantitative analysis, stringent cost controls, demanding collection schedules, and what he calls "my intuitive algorithm" for finding, acquiring, and retaining customers. In a business where the best ideas are quickly appropriated and copied, Providian has managed to stay a couple of steps ahead of the competition by honoring its analytical and intuitive roots.

The late Bill Lear, developer of the Lear Jet, helped launch the modern businessperson's favorite way to travel. He had over 150 other patents to his credit. When asked where he got his ideas for his new products, he said, "First I perceive a need for a product that doesn't exist. I take all the facts I can gather about the subject and put them in my subconscious. Then sometime later I get an intuitive answer which brings the solution into clear focus."

Turner, Mehta, and Lear have one thing in common: they trust their intuition. These business leaders and many others are saying that there is more wisdom in our gut than in the brain. It is by trusting our intuition that we can further develop it.

New discoveries about the brain and its unlimited potential are creating an atmosphere of excitement in leadership, sales training, education, family counseling, and environmental preservation. Perhaps the biggest single reason for the growing acceptance of intuition is necessity. Whether you work in the secretarial pool or on the board of directors, in pharmaceutical research or sales in a drug store, you need to develop and become aware of your intuitive intelligence and employ your gut guidance.

We still have much to learn about this part of our psyche that will give us a competitive advantage in both our personal and in our business life. Meanwhile, we know that intuition cannot be ordered, commanded, implored, or contrived. It comes on its own accord bearing flashes of insight, hunches, and sometimes with a scary conviction. We simply have to recognize it and learn to use it. If we doubt or mistrust the process, we will block its path into our conscious awareness and our positive results will be erratic. If we welcome its input with openness and patience, however, it will become quite dependable, tending to show up at all the right times.

Questions Ignite Intuitive Flashes

One method is to ask questions and then stop thinking about them. We thus delegate the job of coming up with answers to our unconscious mind. First, spend some quality time answering these questions on a conscious level, then take a break. Leave the question or questions alone for awhile. This creates a receptive mind state. Have a notepad handy and be ready to record any insights that surface. Keep in mind there is no telling how rapidly an answer will come. It can be nearly instantaneous or take days or weeks. The key is to put your mind in a receptive mode and catch the moment when the intuitive flash hits. Whether you are preparing for a sales presentation or a board meeting, these questions will help prepare your subconscious to send the right answers. Resolve to divorce the following anti-intuition attitudes that conspire to limit the effectiveness of your gut guidance: pessimism, intolerance of ambiguity, excessive logic, inflexibility, and a deficiency of "do nothing" time.

Thinking Without Thinking

It is important to understand this shift in the decision-making process so that you can be effective in your ability to influence and persuade with integrity. Integrity must be at the core for we are all at war with exploiters and terrorists of the mind. While the dominance of our unconscious, instinctual brain can be quite frightening, it also gives us the power and efficiency of thinking without thinking as described in *Blink* by Malcolm Gladwell.

Gladwell's reference to "blink" confirms the power and efficiency of what I refer to as intuitive intelligence. He explains how experts felt a wave of "intuitive repulsion" when they examined a false Greek statue that was sold to a deceived buyer for $10 million. In just two seconds, or in a single glance, one group of experts knew what took others fourteen months to understand.

Our brain processes information on two different channels to come to the same conclusion. The more traditional, conscious approach is tedious and time-consuming as it is based on gathering information and learned experiences. The adaptive unconscious, however, leaps to conclusions in that it processes lots of information very quickly like a computer. While Gladwell refers to the adaptive unconscious as an apparatus that is capable of making very quick judgments based on very little information, I would disagree that it is little information. It is just not the more obvious, conventional, visual reality that we define as "information."

However, I do agree with his assertion that decisions made very quickly can be every bit as good as decisions made cautiously and deliberately. Because of the primitive nature of information processed by the adaptive unconscious or the instinctual brain, it is crucial that you channel responses with traditional intellect before acting on your impulse. If an idea comes from your gut or heart, run it through your head or intellect. If it originates from your head, run it through your heart before deciding on a course of action. It makes for a balanced decision that is controlled and has direction. The truth is revealed in the decoding or how you interpret and read the information given which is often visceral such as sweating palms, a pounding heart, or butterflies in your stomach.

In *Blink*, Gladwell also refers to "thin-slicing," which he explains as the ability of our unconscious to find patterns in situations and behaviors based on narrow slices of experiences. This accelerated processing of information makes our adaptive unconscious or instinctual brain efficient and thus essential for decision-making in our fast-paced world where every second counts. In fact, our ability to think without thinking, act on our hunches, or decide in a "blink" has saved many lives as demonstrated in the disaster of 9/11. There was no time for a spreadsheet or analysis of the pros and cons. Survival of the fittest is often about who can think without thinking and act fast.

Understanding how the instinctual/intuitive brain receives and processes information is crucial to your success for it is where decisions are made and the roots of power. First of all, it feeds on energy and passion, so give it your all. Don't hold back, although it is important not to overwhelm. Speak the appropriate language which requires that you be versatile and diversified to connect, resonate, and create a bond. I prefer two models of communication. One is HBDI (Herrmann Brain Dominance Inventories) which is based on diverse thinking styles, and the second is the NLP (Neuro-Linguistic Programming) model that incorporates the three sensory modalities: auditory, visual, and kinesthetic.

Since our intuitive/instinctual brain operates much like a young child, you must present information to others as if speaking to a child. First of all, you need to grab their attention with a startling fact, story, or drama. Create experiential learning and participation by incorporating emotion, visuals, and action. Stories well told create sensory impressions, stir emotions, and need to be included but must relate to a point that in turn relates to the world of the customer. Emotions are actually an inner source of energy, information, and influence and with no emotion, there is no motion or action. To get a decision you need to create emotion. In *Selling To The Old Brain*, Renvoisé and Morin present six stimuli that speak directly to their reference of the Old Brain which is the master switch or clearing center for what then goes to the cerebral cortex or the new brain, which I refer to as the creative brain. They present the six stimuli that speak directly to the Old Brain:

Six Stimuli to the Old Brain

1. Self-centered...the center of ME.
2. Solid contrasts such as before/after, slow/fast. Without contrast, the Old Brain enters a state of confusion, which ultimately results in delaying a decision, or worse, making no decision at all.
3. Tangible input: The Old Brain is constantly scanning for what is familiar and friendly; what can be recognized quickly, what is concrete and immutable. It appreciates simple, easy-to-grasp, concrete ideas like "more money," "unbreakable," and "24-hour turn around time."
4. Remembers the beginning and the end, but forgets most everything in between. (With) this short attention span...placing the most important content at the beginning and repeating it at the end is imperative....anything you say in the middle of your delivery will be mostly overlooked.
5. Visual...The optical nerve is physically connected to the Old Brain and is 25 times faster than the auditory nerve. Therefore, the visual channel provides a fast and effective connection to the true decision-maker.
6. Triggered by emotion...emotional reactions create chemical events in your brain that directly impact the way you process and memorize information. In fact, you simply can't remember events and information for anything more than the short-term unless you

experience what some scientists refer to as a strong "emotional cocktail," the result of emotions processed by the brain.

Four Steps to Sales Success

1. Diagnose the PAIN and craft a message that concretely demonstrates to your prospect how you will cure it. Pain is personal – financial – strategic.
2. Differentiate your CLAIMS from those of your competition.
3. Demonstrate the GAIN that your solutions provide to your prospect.
4. Deliver to the OLD BRAIN in a way that has maximum impact.

Most decisions are based on fear and that includes your fear. Disguising your fear is like trying to stop sweating. Pouka, my seven pound black poodle mutt, used to bark at every big dog on the block but somehow knew enough not to attack them. He obviously sensed the bigger dog was not the least bit intimidated by his passionate bark backed up by a minuscule body. If you have no fear of losing the sale and are willing to walk away, in most cases you just marked it sold! The secret is to act with high intention and low attachment so that you don't conduct business like it is a life-threatening event.

Your words should be simple, short, and to the point as people are easily distracted and tune out quickly. When presenting information, hit your delete key repeatedly so that you are not telling but selling.

Using the word "You" is essential because the instinctual brain is self-centered and thus lights up when it hears the word "You." It could care less about your products, your features, or even your benefits unless it directly impacts them. "You" is like the pass code to the instinctual brain. Renvoisé and Morin also present a system involving six message building blocks that are listed below:

Six Message Building Blocks

1. Grabber: Your opening attention getter.
2. Big Picture: The use of visuals speak to the Old Brain
3. Claims: The repetition of unique reasons prospects should buy from you.
4. Proof of Gain: Irrefutable evidence of what prospects will gain from your solution.

5. Handling Objections: Being prepared for rational and not-so-rational objections.

6. Close: Getting positive public feedback and letting your prospects commit to the next steps.

Brain Shortcuts for Mental Misers

People are mental misers. When rushed or pressured to make a decision, people conserve their energies by taking shortcuts in their decision-making; especially since most of us are on information overload. Our minds are on automatic pilot most of the time. We are programmed and conditioned to say "Yes" or "No" to various suggestive cues or persuasive requests.

While new habits and behaviors do create new neuropathways, the new patterns do not replace or destroy the old ones. This is why we tend to be creatures of habit. Both the new and older, established neural highways in the mind actually compete for dominance. An example is the late ABC news anchor Peter Jennings who quit smoking using hypnosis (a method that rewires those nasty behavior patterns nestled in the unconscious mind). The stress of 9/11 caused a brain downshift where his addiction to smoking overrode his conscious desire to be healthy. Although *The Road Less Traveled* is a great book, it is not an indicator of human behavior which prefers taking the old, beaten path of what is familiar.

In general, the conscious mind is focused on the future and is responsive to positive information. It is a single system that is fact-finding and flexible. The unconscious mind is rigid and "now" oriented. It reacts to negative information and is sensitive to pattern changes that are detected by our senses making it multi-systemic. It is prone to fast action with a racetrack mentality as opposed to the conscious, rational mind that prefers to just think things over as in a stroll in the park.

The Environment as a Modifier

An important behavior modifier that is frequently overlooked is one's environment. As I write this book, I gaze over Sunset Lake, and am listening to soothing classical music. Just to the left and the right of my computer are two different stained glass lampshades with sailboats on calming blue waters. Another wall holds a waterfront scene by

Monet and my favorite painting by James Siebert that explodes with energy. I have been writing since morning and it is now past midnight but I don't feel bored or tired after working over 12 hours. You guessed it. My environment nourishes and inspires me. It inspires and affects how I think and make choices. How will you integrate the suggestive powers of environment to improve your mood, your thinking, and to nourish you? How will you create an environment that constructively changes the behaviors and responses of others? When dating, much effort is put into creating a romantic environment and it works until most people get a bit lazy and skip the environmental stuff and then wonder why the love fades.

We are all interconnected and thus influenced by the social and economic environments as well. There is strong circumstantial evidence that social mood, resulting from a strong bear or bull market, also influences the actions of serial killers. What do Richard Speck, the Zodiac Killer, Charles Manson, John Wayne Gacy, Ted Bundy, David Berkowitz (Son of Sam), Wayne Williams, and Gary Ridgeway have in common? According to Robert Prechter in *The Elliott Wave Theorist*, they are all famous serial killers who struck during the wave IV bear market from 1966-1982. Even the massacre of 914 followers of Jim Jones was in 1978—that same time period. The correlations of these and other serial killers to the social mood are significant. For example, Jeffrey Dahmer had killed just once, in June 1978, in the middle of the 1966-1982 bear market. He killed no one for the next nine years, throughout the rising trend, but the very month after it topped out in August 1987, he began a spree of capturing, killing, dismembering, and eating 15 people. This correlation is also demonstrated in social events and the nature of movies released, with torture movies engaging audiences during a bear market. *The Passion of Christ*, one of the most graphic films of all time, became mainstream and a family outing, even though a woman suffered a heart attack and died while viewing it.

My purpose in presenting these patterns is to make you aware of how our instinctual brain is affected by a cultural consciousness and how the moods of the mob may trigger impulsive behaviors and even violence. The instinctual brain also affects selling and buying behaviors and thus, to be effective in peruasion, you must be aware of the delicate dance of all influencing factors.

Change has changed. The velocity of change has changed and thus "instant" influence has become essential for impact in the sales process and in leadership roles. Know that 95 percent of the reasons a person buys or follows involves an unconscious decision. Thus, you must know about more than your product or process, but also about the thinking pattern of the prospect or team member and what is at their emotional core. We decide by emotion and justify it with logic. Words are not just words, but are triggers to symbols and mind impressions that evoke emotions. Remove all obstacles by anticipating any of the objections. By presenting any disadvantages or negatives right at the beginning, you will gain trust and increase rapport: essential elements for being open to your suggested resolutions. If you don't bring up the problems, they will fester in the mind of the customer and create invisible barriers.

Integrity (or lack of) is sniffed out like hounds on a hunt. Integrity is having your thoughts, words, and deeds all in alignment. It is walking your talk and being a person of honor. Only if you honor your words and your promises are you deserving of the prize.

Psychologists Richard Petty and John Cacioppo have labeled the thoughtful and mindless routes to persuasion as central and peripheral. In the central route, the message receiver actively thinks about the message and rationally analyzes all the logic and evidence presented. In the peripheral route, the message receiver spends little time processing the content. The mind activates a decision trigger that tells the receiver to say "Yes" or "No." The triggers are largely emotionally driven, and the receiver relies on simple cues. In *Artful Persuasion*, Harry Mills lays out the two routes to successful persuasion.

Two Routes to Successful Persuasion

Thoughtful Persuasion
- Is motivated to listen and evaluate
- Has high involvement
- Actively processes information

Mindless Persuasion
- Lacks motivation or ability to listen and evaluate
- Has low involvement
- Uses passive processing and automatic decision triggers

- Weighs pros and cons of evidence
- Uses reason and logic
- Has lasting attitude change and is resistant to other changes

- Doesn't use counter arguing and doesn't search for persuasive cues
- Uses little intellectual analysis and is instinct and emotion driven
- Has temporary attitude change and easily changes mind

What people say and think they will do may often have little to do with their actual actions. However, in *The Science of Influence*, Kevin Hogan reports that there are several factors that do predict buying behaviors:

1. Ownership. Once someone possesses something, they perceive it to be more valuable than prior to owning it. Thus, you must get people to try it on. Get your ideas, services, or products in their hands and minds.

2. Mental Images. Create a frame or word picture in their minds that the idea, service, or product is already theirs.

3. Loss Aversion. People will do more to defend what they have than to invest in potential gain. That is why so many people don't quit smoking or other health threatening behaviors until a diagnosis is made and loss of life is pending. It is also why casinos make big money. Instead of accepting a sure loss, people will gamble at an even greater loss with hopes of breaking even.

4. Concept versus Perception. Make your first impression a great impression. We always remember our first love, first car, and first job more than the second one. Our first thoughts become primary and direct following perceptions. In fact, we filter information that does not match our original belief or experience. Prejudices are certainly proof of this theory.

Hogan gives the following example:
>Say the word "blood" five times.
>Continue reading.
>What color does a traffic light have to be for you to proceed?
>Did you say "red?"
>If so, go back and read it again.

Perceptions and impressions are particularly important in the job search. When people go for an interview there is always the question of whether it is to their advantage to be the first or last person interviewed. The answer is, "It all depends." The findings Hogan reports is that the brain tends to remember that which happens first and last in sequences, events, and life in general. The key factor may be the elapsed time between the events. The shorter the elapsed time, the better it is to go first, but opt to go last if there is a long lapse in time. If you are a middle child, you may not appreciate the fact that yes, things do get lost in the middle.

Resistance: Cognitive and Knee-Jerk

While most sales people are focused on sweetening the pot by increasing the value to make the offer irresistible, the flip side to increase influence is to reduce the resistance. Hogan discusses the two kinds of resistance. The first is a cognitive reactance or knee-jerk reaction to whatever may seem to appear to be a threat to our personal choices and freedoms. Some seem to have "no" hardwired into their brains and continually resist because that simply is what they have always done. This may be a situation of delayed adolescence, the terrible two stage, or just a defense to telemarketing calls.

The other resistance demonstrated is because of an anticipated regret of complying or not complying with a request. People are reluctant to sell a lottery ticket just after purchase. The anticipation of regret believing it could be the winning ticket causes them to resist any such suggestion. Basic reasons for resistance are usually due to no rapport or opportunity. It may also be due to the wrong person or wrong time.

Checklist for Resistance

1. They don't like or trust you (no rapport)
2. They don't need or want what you offer (no opportunity)
3. They don't have a sense of urgency (wrong time)
4. They don't have the money available (no resource)
5. They don't have the authority to make the decision (wrong person)

To increase compliance, we must quickly move people beyond the unconscious fight/flight reactions of the instinctual brain and get them to focus on anticipated regrets that are on the conscious, cerebral level and thus controllable. With the enlightenment of creative, logical thinking, the instinctual reactionary responses can be overruled and progress can be made.

Obviously fear can be a powerful factor in promoting compliance. As Willy Sutton, the infamous bank robber and outlaw in the 1930s once said, "You can get more done with a kind word and a gun than you can with a kind word alone." I certainly would not advocate violence, but there is obviously some truth to his philosophy. Fear does motivate but only while the threat exists. However, hearing the same warning or threat repeatedly dilutes the punch as the brain learns to tune it out. Just instilling fear such as telling people cigarette smoking kills will not alter behavior. This must be followed up with a strategy or step-by-step plan for change to take place. People need tools to change. In sales, you must also suggest a clear plan of action.

Alignment: Influence with Integrity

That action, however, must be laced with integrity. Integrity is having your thoughts, words, and deeds all in alignment. It is walking your talk and being a person of honor. Influence without integrity is abusive and manipulative and thus not integrity. In his biography *Straight Up*, James Ramsey Ullman writes about a young mountain climber, John Harlin, who died at age 30 while trying to climb the Eiger Mountain—straight up. Although you may associate "straight up" with how you order a drink, it is also a way to climb a mountain and live your life. All of the techniques and tactics, skills and strategies presented in this book must be exercised with integrity. At the core, influence and persuasion is about honor and respect in relationships, for no one climbs Success Mountain alone.

Persuasion Tactics

- Keep it short and simple. (*That's* short and simple.)

- Limit choices. Too many choices cause people to freeze and become confused. A confused mind says "No."

- Develop "moodifiers" by creating a supportive environment.

- Create ownership to increase perceived value. Let your language suggest that the product is already theirs.

- Create the greatest impact and impression by knowing when to be first and when to be last. If the time lag is long, last is best.

- Move people from resistance to compliance by knowing where to pitch the ball—to their instinctual brain, emotional brain, or creative mind.

- Don't just tell people what to do, but also provide a step-by step plan for desired action and change.

- Practice integrity. If you exercise any of the information and skills in this book without integrity, please burn the book immediately and forget every word you read.

Epilogue
Be A Class Act

Character is like a tree and reputation is like its shadow.
The shadow is what we think of it; the tree is the real thing.
Abraham Lincoln

Although I have presented numerous techniques and persuasion strategies, more than any system or ideology, serving the people must come first. Integrity must be at the core of influence. Such power in the hands of an evil tyrant is potential devastation to humankind. Contrary to public belief, it was not Hitler's charisma that created compliance and a blind obedience but the herd mentality as explained in the Principle of Social Consensus. If everybody is doing it, we not only begin to tolerate it, we accept and eventually worship it. I remember when chewing gum in school was grounds for expulsion. Today we're relieved if kids don't bring guns to school. Our expectations and social norms, unfortunately, have shifted drastically.

Adaptation is necessary for the survival of all species, but it also gives permission for social evils. Malcolm Gladwell refers to such social epidemics as a word-of-mouth epidemic illustrated by the midnight ride of Paul Revere. Whether it is eating at a restaurant, seeing a movie, or buying a computer, more than an ad or any kind of advertising, it is the suggestion and experiences of another or word-of-mouth that most influences our behavior. While we should seek consensus, we should never be ruled by it.

Leadership is also managing and measuring perceptions. It is about influence, which can be positive or negative. Obviously coercion, intimidation, and manipulation are negative and create distrust and suspicion. The give-and-take of negotiation is neutral, and the most positive influence is persuasion, education, and inspiration. With mutual respect and alignment, influence with integrity forms alliances and partnerships that achieve excellence by making a difference in the global community. Motivation is essential to effective leadership and without influence there is no motivation which is turning people on, inspiring, and getting more than 100% from a personal relationship. Transparency or authentic openness to others about one's feelings, beliefs, and actions nurtures integrity and trust, the universal connector. Even more than being in alignment, we must be attuned to those we are leading. People need to see, feel, and touch the value and the vision of the organization to make these abstractions meaningful. To determine if you are a true leader, answer this simple question: "When you lead—will they follow?"

Ultimately, the most meaningful act of responsibility is to first control our own mental state, to live our values, and walk our talk. Since the onset of terrorism, values are no longer synonymous with virtue; for terrorists are consistent with their values and unfortunately do walk their talk. Integrity is defined as upholding high moral principles of right and wrong, but right and wrong is in the eyes of the beholder and by definition is not absolute or universal. Therefore, integrity must come from a loving and compassionate heart that out of honor and respect serves and enhances the well being of the other which Dan Sullivan, cofounder of the Strategic Coach, Inc., would define as a "class act." Dan states that, "In every society, there are 'Human Benchmarks'—certain individuals whose behavior becomes a model for everyone else—shining examples that others admire and emulate. We call these individuals 'class acts.'" They seem to attract other people with class into their sphere of influence.

A friend and class act I so much respect for his authenticity and integrity is Jack Canfield, coauthor of the *Chicken Soup for the Soul* series and author of *The Success Principles* wherein he presents Dan Sullivan's Class Act Model which I have summarized as follows:

Class Act Characteristics

Live by your own highest standards. Class acts liberate themselves by establishing personal standards of thinking and behavior that are more demanding and exacting than those of conventional society. They are consciously chosen, established, and applied…

Maintain dignity and grace under pressure. There are three aspects of this characteristic. The first is imperturbability in the face of chaos…The second is a calmness that gives courage…The third is a quality of certainty…

Focus and improve the behavior of others. Because a class act individual is a good role model, other people around them begin thinking and acting at a level that surprises both themselves and others…

Operate from a larger, inclusive perspective. Because class acts are in touch with their own humanity, they have a deeper understanding and compassion for the humanity of others…

Increase the quality of every experience. Class act individuals have the ability to transform seemingly insignificant situations into something enjoyable, meaningful, and memorable because of their conscious thinking and actions. They are creators rather than consumers, and they constantly enrich the lives of others by introducing greater beauty, significance, uniqueness, and stimulation into every experience…

Counteract meanness, pettiness, and vulgarity. The hallmarks of this characteristic are courtesy, respect, appreciation, gratitude, and generosity of spirit…

Take responsibility for actions and results. Class act individuals are accountable when others hide; they tell the truth about their failures, and they transform defeats into progress…

Strengthen the integrity of all situations. Class act individuals are always establishing and achieving larger goals that require them to constantly grow and develop as well as add increasing value to the world...

Expand the meaning of being human... In pushing boundaries for themselves, they do the same for others by giving them new freedom to express their uniqueness in the world...

Increase the confidence and capabilities of others. Class acts are energy creators rather than energy drainers.

Influence with integrity gives you the tools to be a class act. When your skills to influence increase, your impact on others is stronger and thus your responsibility grows along with your power, for the primary outcome of organizational life is the development of people. When you influence without awareness of the other person's needs and outcomes, then you are influencing in the dark and may be unintentionally guilty of manipulation. These powerful tools and techniques are neither innocent nor guilty, but are neutral for only human beings have intentions and integrity. As we radiate the purpose-driven life, we create resonance and the authentic power of influence to create a compassionate culture. How one uses his or her access to power best determines true character as proclaimed by Abraham Lincoln:

> "Nearly all men can stand adversity,
> but if you want to test a man's character,
> give him power."

Index

ABOUT THE AUTHOR

Providing an ROI (Return on Innovative Intelligence), Edie Raether is an internationally recognized authority on the neuroscience of success and breakthrough thinking as a business strategy and the currency of the future. With expertise in emotional and intuitive intelligence, innovation, and influence, her revolutionary concepts—MindShift™, FutureThink™, LeaderShift™, and TeamThink™—engage whole-brain thinking for personal renewal, strategic positioning, and organizational change. As a keynote speaker, Edie has empowered over 3,000 professional associations and Fortune 500 companies such as IBM, General Motors, JC Penney, S.C. Johnson, Oscar Mayer, the Marriott, ASTD, and MPI.

Edie is the author of *Why Cats Don't Bark, Sex for the Soul,* and *Winning! How Winners Think-What Champions Do.* In addition to numerous audio and video Change Mastery programs, Edie has also coauthored several inspirational and business anthologies.

Edie is an expert resource for hundreds of publications such as *The Wall Street Journal, USA Today, Prevention, Selling Power, INC magazine and Reuters.* Edie has also shared the platform with such celebrities as Tom Brokaw, Patch Adams, Art Linkletter, and Bob Hope.

A behavioral science expert, Edie has over thirty years of experience as a human asset manager and psychotherapist. She has also been a college professor and talk show host with ABC. Edie is the recipient of various Who's Who's and the CSP (Certified Speaking Professional) award which is the highest earned designation awarded by the National Speakers Association to fewer than eight percent of its membership.

Changing the Way the World Thinks…One Mind at a Time

For more information on Edie's speaking, coaching, and training programs, other books or her Change Mastery programs available on tape or CD, please visit her website at www.raether.com or contact her office:

Performance PLUS
4717 Ridge Water Court
Holly Springs, NC 27540
919-557-7900 or 1-888-Raether
Email: info@edieraether.com
www.raether.com